NONE TO GIVE AWAY

NONE
TO GIVE
AWAY

By Elsie Doig Townsend

CHAPTER ONE

I had been a rural school teacher in the little valley surrounded by mountains in western Montana. Then, when I was practically an old maid, I married one of the ranchers—Jim Doig—definitely a bachelor. My habits must have been as difficult to adjust to as his were for he often said grimly, "Getting married didn't make you any less an old maid."

Nevertheless we brought forth five children in less than four years, one single and two sets of twins. When the last twins were born—on the Fourth of July—my husband put his hand over his face, groaned, and muttered a few choice epithets that cowboys toss at cantankerous cows.

I remember that I cried all night. The doctor, hearing of my tears, came into the room and said sternly, "Mrs. Doig, what in the world are you crying about?"

"If I'd known it was twins again, I wouldn't have had that last one," I said and began to sob again.

"Nature has a way of taking care of that," he said. He grinned as he patted my shoulder and left.

Hordes of people came to the hospital to view me—to gloat over me, I insisted. The nurses counted up to ninety-nine visitors, and quit counting. After all, not many people had their children in litters—that was for animals. The visitors were from the neighboring ranches, as far as forty miles away. They would stand around and laugh.

"Wonder if she'll have them in quadruplets next time?"

"Ought to call them Pete and Repeat."

"No, Kate and Duplicate."

"Two little firecrackers on the Fourth of July."

"Jim always did like to put two calves on one cow!"

Oh, I knew that the joking was in good humor, but I was irked. I wondered about our little winter house. It would bulge at the seams with this increase of two more children. The house was made of logs. I had helped my husband peel them and put them in place. We had built everything ourselves. Every other year we had added a room. But, as my husband so aptly expressed it, "I just can't win. Every time I add one room, Elsie goes and has two kids."

While I was in the hospital, after the birth of the babies, Jim came to visit with me as often as he could, but between riding herd on all the cattle on the ranch and taking care of three small children, he had his hands full.

"How are the youngsters?" I would ask eagerly.

"Okay," he always answered. I would have to pry any other bits of information out of him. His Scotch blood showed itself in his succinct remarks. He joked about his Scottish instincts. "I talk through my nose," he would explain laughingly, "to save the wear and tear on my teeth."

"Now, come on, give," I would coax, and he would tell me a few incidents.

"The housekeeper had a bit of trouble yesterday. You know that open fifty-pound sack of flour in the storeroom? The twins sneaked out of their naps yesterday. She didn't miss 'em for about an hour—found 'em sittin' on the floor, pouring flour over their heads. Yeah, about twenty-five pounds of it. I picked 'em up and shook 'em like puppy dogs. Tried to wash their hair. Doggondest mess of dough you ever saw."

He stopped to laugh, but I did not think it was funny.

"Don't worry . . . the housekeeper got it all cleaned out finally." He reached for his old Stetson. "Got to go, sweet," he said as he stood. "Shippin' a few carloads of fat dries to

Chicago this week. The boys are roundin' up the cattle in the corrals on top of the mountain right now." He kissed me and was gone.

I was homesick to see my brood and daily begged the doctor to let me go home. He hesitated, since the babies had been so premature and were in the incubator. At last he consented.

"You can go home tomorrow. You are stewing more here in the hospital than you would at home. All this fussing is going to curdle your milk. And I do want you to nurse these babies."

Jim came to the hospital to get me. The children hung onto their father and eyed me suspiciously, as if I were a stranger.

"Never mind, sweet," he said knowingly, "they'll soon get over it."

The two baskets, with a baby in each one, and five of us besides that, crowded our car as we drove up the valley toward our home in the mountains. And the visitors continued to come. They brought many gifts, which I piled on the top of the piano, on the dining room table, everywhere. I was sure that they felt sorry for me, and this was a way to show their concern.

The children and I got acquainted again, but they showed no real curiosity about the tiny twin babies; they just were not interested. Beverly had always been an independent child. Now a three-year-old, she went on about her play, except when I called her to help me. The older twins, Margie and Marilyn, were completely satisfied with each other's company; they played together for hours. They even developed a sort of language of their own. Margie learned to say her words almost as plainly as we did. Marilyn was slower. One day I noticed that Margie was saying "op" for "yes."

"Margie, can't you say 'Yes'?" I asked, stopping her as she passed me, carrying her teapot of water out for mud pies.

She stood still, slopping water down the front of her dress.

"Ess," she said as she raised her blue eyes to me.

"Then why do you say 'Op'?"

"Mennin"—her name for Marilyn—"say 'Op'; I say 'Op,' " she answered, and trotted off to her mud pies.

That settled that!

The children treated me as if I were a necessity, but they worshiped their father. Much of the day he was off riding over the hills on horseback, taking care of the cattle, but he spent his free hours with the children.

One evening he was turning the crank of the cream separator out in the milk room. Running back and forth from that room to the kitchen where I was working, the children tied us together with their chatter.

"Mama, Daddy say I'm a humbug," Margie chattered.

"Daddy say I'm humbug," Marilyn echoed.

"Tell Daddy he's a humbug," I said absentmindedly.

Back they ran to the milk room.

"Daddy, you a humbug," they would chorus, and Jim, letting go the handle of the cream separator for a second or two, would swing one twin off the ground and set her down, again grabbing the handle and beginning to turn it.

"Swing me too," the other would say. And he would, as soon as he had the separator going at top speed again.

Beverly seriously helped her father change cream cans, carried to him the water for rinsing, watched his every move. She adored her father.

The tie of our family was made of a strong cord of love.

CHAPTER TWO

Three months later, early on an October morning, Jim got up from the breakfast table and said, "I'm going to help Alden Crowall cut out a hundred fat steers to ship. They're up here in the mountain pasture, so I'll drive the old Ford over there and ride one of Alden's horses. Guess I won't wear my boots. That nail in the heel hurts my foot. Got to have them repaired."

He disentangled the older twins from around his legs, tousled their hair a bit, and said to Beverly who stood nearby, "Help your mother, will you?" Then he kissed us all and was gone.

I began the familiar routine of helping Eunice, the housekeeper, pick up the dishes and make the beds, preparatory to bathing the little babies. The air was very cool outside early in the morning. The children played in whichever room I was working. When I put a pan of water on the table and brought one of the twin babies from the bedroom, the little girls stopped their play and gathered around the table. It was always fun to watch this bathing process. They loved to touch the petal-soft skin of the little hands and feet, to help shake on the powder and rub it gently. As soon as I had one baby bathed and dressed and wrapped in a blanket, I called Eunice to bathe the other baby as I nursed this one.

It was a quiet morning. The sun peeping over the side of Ross's Peak, the highest mountain on our east, poured its warmth into the valley and took the chill out of the air. The children went outside to play. I heard their voices as I passed the open door and the windows.

Suddenly a horse and rider galloped up to the house. I stepped to the door as he swung off his horse, tossed down the reins, and ran up to me. It was Ronnie Crowall.

"Elsie," he said breathlessly, "Jim's been hurt. Dad says to call an ambulance—quick."

Mechanically I turned to the telephone on the wall and rang, then asked our local switchboard operator to let me talk to "the ambulance people." As I waited for her to make the connection, I turned to Ronnie and said, "Where shall I have it come?"

"Right here, Dad said, to this house, and you can bring it to the pasture—over by the west fence on section seventeen—you know, come in the lower gate, by that big chokecherry clump."

He was on his horse and gone as quickly as he had come. I stood numbly waiting for some rising emotion to come— some uncontrolled hysteria of fear. But it did not come. All that I experienced was a kind of deadness, as if the thinking-feeling part of my body had ceased to exist. It took years for me to understand that that was what happened right then.

I moved back and forth around the house, unable to concentrate on anything. The children followed me about and asked questions. I answered them as unemotionally as if this were an ordinary occurrence. In about thirty minutes Ronnie came again.

"Elsie," he called, not even getting off his horse, "Dad says to call the doctor, and tell him to hurry," and again his horse's heels threw up a flurry of dust as he wheeled and took off.

In a moment I was talking to Dr. Kittern. "Jim's been hurt," I said as soon as I had told him who I was. "I've called the ambulance, but will you come up to the ranch right away? Come to the house, and I'll go with you to where Jim is." I gave him directions for finding our place.

Again I moved about the rooms, picking up clothes and toys, putting them away, completely unfeeling. "This is the end," I kept mumbling to myself, "the end."

When I looked at Eunice I saw the deep concern mirrored in her eyes, but she did not try to "make" conversation. In less time than it seemed possible for a car to cover the many miles from Bozeman, the doctor arrived.

"I'm going with him," I said to Eunice, and explained to her where to send the ambulance. "I'll have Ronnie posted at the gate to guide it in."

Without getting out of the car, the doctor pushed open the door for me. I got in, and he started the motor.

"Do you know how he's hurt, Mrs. Doig?" he asked after I had given directions for driving to the pasture.

"No," I said, "but Alden is not one to panic, so I know it's very bad."

And then we did not talk, except when I added details of directions. As we came across the pasture, we saw the clump of men and saddled horses huddled about something on the ground. They heard us and moved enough so that through the opening I could see Jim. We came closer and I was out of the car and running to the prone figure before the doctor had stopped the motor. Jim moved restlessly, flipping off the blanket someone had wrapped about him. His cowboy hat lay a few feet away. There was a smudge of dirt on his forehead. I brushed it off as I squatted on the ground beside him. He moaned as he tossed back and forth.

"Try to keep him quiet," the doctor said. I looked up to see him there beside me. Expertly the doctor's hands moved over Jim's body, feeling for broken bones. He shook his head.

"A head injury, I think. We must keep him quiet. Speak to him, Mrs. Doig. Call him by name. Your voice will reach him if anything can."

"Jim," I said and took one of his hands. "Jim, you must lie still. Can you hear me, Jim?"

His eyes were closed. There was no response, but for a few moments he lay quiet.

"Could we take him in your car?" I asked the doctor.

"No—we must not move him till the ambulance comes. Try to keep the blanket over him."

"Alden," I said, as I knelt there holding Jim's hands, "how did it happen?"

"Well, you know, since that rain the ground's muddy down here. Guess his horse slipped—over there—see?" and he pointed to torn-up turf, "and threw Jim right over his head. Never knew Jim not to kick free from a falling horse before. Must have been because he wasn't wearing his cowboy boots. Jim landed on his head—right there where he is. Never made a sound. I was close—so was Ronnie."

We heard a roar of a motor.

"Here comes the ambulance," someone called. It moved slowly over the rough ground until it stopped within a few feet of us.

Skillfully the men of the ambulance lifted Jim, put him on a stretcher, and carried him into the waiting vehicle. I started to get in too.

"No, Mrs. Doig," the doctor said, "you'd better ride with me," and he took me to his car. With the docility of the benumbed, I obeyed.

We followed the ambulance as closely as we could, but it went ahead of us and was out of sight by the time we reached the paved road beyond Belgrade. At one time I looked at the speedometer of the car. The needle pointed to ninety miles an hour. And still the ambulance beat us to the hospital. The doctor led the way to the X-ray room. Jim was already there, lying on the table. Nurses and interns were trying to hold him quiet so that they could take the X rays.

"Take off his gloves and help us make him lie still," the doctor said to me.

I moved close to the table to obey him. The nurses turned Jim's head this way and that, up and down, taking pictures from every angle and position. Suddenly the thought came to me, My father died just four years ago from a fall and brain damage. Jim's father, years ago, fell and died of a fractured skull. It can't happen again. It can't be a third. . . .

"We're taking him to his room, Mrs. Doig," the doctor said. "Would you go to the front office and give the necessary information for his admittance?"

With the same mechanical obedience I went out into the hall and took the elevator to the front office. Again there was that pounding in my head, "This is it, Elsie . . . you must face it . . . don't give in to your emotions now."

By the time I reached Jim's room, the nurses had him in a bed there. The white sheet pulled so smoothly up to his chin contrasted with his tanned skin. He began to move restlessly. The nurses lifted his arms from under the sheet and bedspread. He turned onto his side, then flopped onto his back.

"Try to keep him quiet. He must be quiet." It was the doctor standing just inside the door.

I took one of Jim's hands. He held tightly to my hand as I spoke to him.

"Do that again," the doctor said quickly. "I think his eyelids flicked."

"Jim, lie very quiet. Can you hear me?" Probably I imagined it, but I thought he squeezed my hand.

"Stay here with him, Mrs. Doig. I want to go look at the X rays."

I stood by the bed, holding tightly to Jim's hand, smoothing his hair from his forehead, speaking to him whenever he began to move. The doctor returned.

"No broken bones; no fractured skull," he said, "no evidence of pressure, but it must be brain injury. We'll do a spinal puncture."

I didn't have to be told to leave the room. As I walked down the hall several nurses spoke to me, calling me by name. After all, I had come here every two years to have babies—three times. I wandered to the little reception room on that floor and leafed through a magazine. I read the words, line by line, but no conception of their meaning entered my mind. My brain could not grasp any ideas. It seemed dead, lifeless. A nurse came into the room.

"Oh, Mrs. Doig," she said, "how are all those twins? Two sets of them, aren't there?"

The children! I must go to them. But how could I get home? I went to the main office and stood a moment trying to think what to do. Then I saw Alden unfolding his long body from a chair in the reception room.

"Followed you here. Been waiting. Can you tell me anything?" he asked.

I shook my head.

"Can I do anything?" he asked.

"Oh—oh, yes. Take me home so that I can see the children and get my car."

"Sure thing," he said and put on his battered Stetson. "Car's out front."

We did not talk on the long drive out to the ranch. There just wasn't anything to say. What could one talk about? My world seemed to have dissolved completely. Only a vacancy was left—in my head, in my mind.

Automatically I thanked Alden as I got out of the car and went into the house. His eyes looked troubled, but he did not express his thoughts. He did not need to.

The children met me at the door. I stooped to put my arms around them.

"Daddy's been hurt. He's in the hospital. Mommy's got to go back to him right away." I must not arouse their emotions unnecessarily, but I must explain to them.

Then I hurried to the babies' baskets, took up Jimmy, and began to nurse him. I tried to sit quietly and tell Eunice some of the details and give her directions for the children.

"You know how to make up the formula for the babies, Eunice? Make up double the amount we usually do for supplementary feeding. I may not be back for a while."

Putting Jimmy in his basket, I took up Joanie and nursed her as I talked to the children.

"Daddy was riding the horse, and the horse fell down and hurt Daddy."

"Did the horse get hurt too?" Beverly asked.

"No—just Daddy."

"Where is he hurt?"

"His head. Doctor's trying to make him well." I must not transmit my fears to these little girls.

Laying the sleeping baby down, I kissed Beverly and the older twins. They did not cry, but their eyes were big and they looked lonely. Closing my mind to all this, I went quickly to the car and drove back to the hospital. Approaching Jim's room, I was suddenly filled with revulsion. I can't go in there, I thought. I can't look at him. I know I can't. But I walked quietly in and went to the head of his bed.

"He's been terribly restless," the nurse said. "One of us has to hold him down most of the time."

"Jim," I said, taking one of his hands, then louder, "Jim." His grasp on my hand was firm and definite. "You must lie still. Now I'm going to talk to you." I began to speak—in almost a monotone—about the children, about the ranch, about the cow dogs. He became quiet. I stopped talking and waited. In a few minutes he began to toss about in the bed. Again I talked to him. This went on for hours. In the evening the doctor came in. He had nothing to tell me.

"Only a trace of blood in the spinal fluid."

"Any indication of surgery to remove pressure?" I asked.

"No. We'll have to wait. I have two special nurses for him. But you'll have to stay here as much as you can. Your voice is the only thing he responds to. Somehow it penetrates, I think." And he was gone.

I felt completely alone. If I had someone! My sister, Irene, in Whitehall! I would call her. I fumbled in my purse for coins and searched for a telephone. Of course I could not think how to reach her in the evening, now, and her office was closed. But the operator kept following my suggestions until I was talking to Irene. I explained Jim's accident. Being a nurse, she understood quickly.

"I'll come to be with you as soon as I can," she promised. "In the meantime, there's Harry. I'll call him."

Harry! I had not thought of him . . . Irene's friend on the college faculty. . . . Of course! Harry had spent many weekends at the ranch. He and Jim had talked for hours. I went back to the room and found Jim moaning and throwing himself about the bed. This time it was more difficult to quiet him.

Harry came, and I told him all that I knew. We talked desultorily. The long hours of the night dragged on. Sometimes I went out into the hall and walked around. Once a nurse came to me, put her arm around me and said, "Mrs. Doig, have you had anything to eat?"

"No, I guess I haven't. But I really am not hungry."

"Well, we're going to the commissary right now, you and I," she said, "and eat."

As we ate she talked to me—about the hospital, about the children, about everything except Jim. Then she went with me to his room. It was getting late. I persuaded Harry to go. About four o'clock in the morning Jim became quiet. The special nurse beckoned to me.

"Come with me," she said, as soon as we were out in the hall. She took me to a room, empty except for one bed. "There," she said as she pulled back the bedspread and sheet. "Now crawl up on that bed and try to sleep. I'll waken you if I need you."

With very little protesting I took off my shoes and climbed up onto the cool white bed and dropped my head onto the pillow. I must have slept, for when the nurse began shaking me, the daylight was bright in the room.

"Can't keep him quiet at all," she said, and I followed her down the hall and into the room where Jim lay.

His face with its dark shadow of a beard looked gaunt on the pillow. He rolled back and forth in the bed, pulling the bedclothes with him. Gently I passed my hand over his face. He took my hand, held it firmly. But it became more and more difficult to quiet him. When the doctor came in mid-morning, I asked him what could be done.

"We'll give him some morphine," he said.

In a few moments all of Jim's activity had stopped. He became so still that I called to the nurse. She took his pulse, listened for his breathing. I could tell by her expression that something was wrong. There was no rise and fall of the bedcovers over his chest. He lay completely passive. In a few minutes the nurse, who had gone out of the room, returned, followed by the doctor. He gave Jim a shot—a powerful stimulant—to which there was almost instantaneous response. Soon Jim was breathing normally—and again he was restless. The day wore on.

The thought came to my mind that I had not nursed the babies for twenty-four hours and still I had no milk. But it seemed unimportant. I telephoned Eunice about the children.

That evening Dr. Kittern brought another doctor into the room. Carefully they examined Jim. Taking one foot from under the covers, the doctor tapped it gently with a rubber mallet. No response. He moved the mallet across the sole of the foot, first with a soft movement, then with pressure. Still no response. He tried the other foot. Jim jerked and squirmed.

"Paralysis on one side," the doctor muttered. "First his speech and now this."

Something cold and sharp seemed to cut into my stomach and tear on up into my chest. I knew what the doctors were trying to prepare me for. They went away and I said to the nurse, "I must go home to see my children. I'll be back in a few hours."

Carefully I drove the miles to our house. When I opened the door and saw the three little girls looking up at me, their forlorn expressions almost frightened me. I talked to them as I moved to the bedroom to see the babies. Eunice followed me, answering my questions before I could form them.

"Babies doing fine on the formula. Of course you know they've been taking one or two bottles at night now for quite a while. Everything's okay. Don't you worry about us. Alden sent a boy to milk the cows and take care of everything."

I knew now why I had had to come home—to gain strength to face whatever I had to meet. Here I had found my need for standing strong. From these children I could gain determination to go back to Jim—to try to will him to live. We had to have him.

Nothing tore me apart so completely as looking into my children's eyes and seeing their desolation as I had to leave them alone. With my jaws gritted so tightly that my neck ached, I turned away from the three little girls and hurried back to the hospital.

I telephoned Jim's brothers, his mother, his sister. One by one they came. His mother was so overcome with emotion that we could not let her stay long at one time in his room. Dr. Kittern called in a brain surgeon, Dr. Sigmund. I talked on the telephone to my brother, a doctor also. He advised me to have the specialist consider brain surgery. I talked to Dr. Sigmund about it.

"We can try it—last resort, you understand. But the patient is becoming more and more paralyzed," he said.

After the three doctors consulted, Dr. Kittern came to me.

"If you give your consent, we'll operate this afternoon. It has been almost four days now. The longer he is unconscious, the more damage there is likely to be."

"Is there any hope otherwise?" I asked and looked directly into the doctor's eyes.

For a moment he said nothing. Then he said slowly,

"None, unless he continued to live—a hopeless idiot, unconscious, paralyzed."

"Jim wouldn't want that," I said. "We must try surgery. Will you explain it to his folks?"

He nodded and I went out into the hall, to walk back and forth, my hands clenched tightly, my mind trying to grasp it all.

At 1:30 the nurses wheeled Jim out of the room on his bed and down the hall to the elevator. I followed the bed, but could not get into the elevator with it and the nurses. I ran up the stairs to the operating floor and followed his bed to the double doors that were swung open by the waiting nurses. They pushed his bed through, and I stood leaning my head against the closed glass doors.

The doctors in operating gowns stepped into the hall. Dr. Kittern came toward me. "It will take a long time," he said. "I'll let you know of any discoveries or developments as soon as I can." The nurses opened the double glass doors, and the doctors went into the operating room.

Jim's sister, Anna, had come up behind me.

"Come," she said softly. "Let's go out on the porch and wait."

But out there it was a babel of sounds. Several relatives were talking together—some explaining to those who had just come. I walked to the railing to look up at the majestic mountain peaks south of us, glowing with the light of the afternoon sun. One of my sisters-in-law followed me over there.

"Elsie, why don't you try praying?" she said, as she flipped her cigarette away and puffed out a cloud of smoke.

For a second I was so angry I was afraid to speak. What could I say? As if every breath hadn't been a prayer, for all these days and nights! An agony of beseeching, of begging, imploring, asking—of trying to understand, trying to reach out to know the will of the Master!

Mumbling something, I fled to the other side of the porch where I paced my little portion of the enclosure. After two hours, someone came to tell me that Jim was still alive. Later—much later—Dr. Kittern came.

"I can't tell you much," he said. "We found the cerebrum swollen and inflamed. We removed a bit of spinal fluid from under the dura. This is all I know."

That night Jim's temperature climbed to 109 degrees. About midnight someone—a nurse I think—gave me some pills. They must have been powerful. At four o'clock in the morning, Jim's brother Angus woke me to say that Jim was dead. Harry was there with him too.

"Will you take me home, Harry?" I asked.

"In a few moments," he answered. "But Elsie, there are some arrangements that must be made immediately. What funeral home?"

I named one.

"The doctor asks if he may perform a postmortem."

I could not speak.

"Elsie, you know how Jim always wanted to know what was the cause of death—of any of his animals. Besides, perhaps the doctors could discover something that might help to save someone else's life."

"It's all right," I said. "Tell them to go ahead."

It must be the drug they gave me, I thought, making me so numb and unfeeling. Without a tremor I went through all the details. Then Harry took me to the car, and we drove home. It was very dark. In the sky not even a faint outline of the mountains was visible. Suddenly I felt completely deserted. The tears began to pour down my face, and I cried convulsively the rest of the way home. Then I

23

became passive. Suddenly I said, "How can I tell the children?"

"You'll find a way, Elsie. I know you'll be able to do this, because that's the kind of person you are."

I bowed my head.

It was almost daylight when we stopped before the house. I went in, stood a minute, then walked on into the bedroom where the little girls slept. They awakened and came to me. With the three of them in my lap and my arms, I sat on the edge of the bed and said quietly, "Your daddy's gone to heaven, children."

"When is he coming back?"

"He can't come back."

"Is he still hurting?"

"No, he'll not be sick anymore."

"Can we see Daddy again?"

"Yes, some day we'll see him, but not for a long time. Right now, you children must help me to live so that we can see him again."

Looking through the open door into the other bedroom at the baskets of the little babies and holding the three girls closely in my arms, I drew from them the courage, the strength, the need to go on.

CHAPTER THREE

I had thought I was abused, having had so many children all at once, had thought I was busy. Now I did not even have time to grieve, except at night, when I spent hours walking up and down the road by our house.

Kind neighbors offered to help me with the cattle, but I knew it was not possible for me to take care of the babies and manage a ranch. I knew nothing but schoolteaching. I could hardly read a brand, had never ridden anything but the gentle saddle horses, got lost if I rode alone over two miles from the ranch house unless I was on a road, could not stand to watch the branding or dehorning. It was useless to attempt the job.

By this time it was the middle of October. Something must be done about the cattle. One morning soon after Jim's funeral Alden Crowall drove up to the house and said abruptly, "Elsie, what do you want done with the cattle? Time to round up the steers and get them sold. Got to do something with all those calves. Have you made up your mind yet?"

I shook my head. "Give me a few days, will you, Alden?"

"Sure thing." Alden pushed back his Stetson and reached for one of his cigarettes—"coffin nails," he always called them. "Wasn't tryin' to rush you. Just wanted you to know that we'll all get together and bring the cattle out as soon as you give us the word."

For several days I pondered over the problem whenever I could find time to think. Jim had always sold his stock to buyers, dealing directly with them. He was "Scotch" in his dickering, kept up on the facts about market prices, drove a close deal. But I had never taken any part in this. One night I had a very real dream that was so clear and distinct I could almost feel that it had happened. Jim came to me in the dream.

"Oh, Jim," I cried out, "you've come back to me."

"Yes, sweet. I had to return to tell you what to do with the cattle. Now let Alden and the neighbors help you round up the cattle and take them to the stock sales in Bozeman as soon as you can."

"But you never wanted to sell cattle at the stock ring," I answered, puzzled.

"I know, I know, but you can't make the deals with the buyers as I did. This is the best way for you."

He started to leave and I clung to him.

"Don't go. Why did you come back to me if you are only going to go again?"

"You were worried about the cattle, so I had to come to help you."

He kissed me good-bye and was gone. I awoke sobbing, but when I had quieted down I understood the dream. As soon as I could I talked to Alden. He nodded as I told him what I wanted to do. Rubbing the bald spot on the top of his head, he began to talk of details.

"We'll bring the fat two-year-old steers and sell them first, all in a lump. Then we'll put that bunch of heifers that are bred for calving next spring in the next selling. The cows and the bulls will be last. Guess it's a good thing Jim sold the steer calves earlier this fall. The heifer calves that he kept will make a good showing—top stuff, specially picked out. Think we'd better gather the cattle at the corrals near the ranch house instead of up on top near Section 18, push them through the loading chute into trucks, and take them into Bozeman. Let's see . . . your brand's the Lazy H N;

Jim's the N hanging H. Any of the old 7-Bar U cattle of Jim's mother's left in the herd yet?"

I was nodding and shaking my head at the proper intervals. We talked of brands, brands of our neighbors on the south. Alden mentioned several riders that could spend a week or more at the ranch to round up and cut out the cattle.

"Don't forget, Alden, someone'll have to take two days and go down to Clarkston on the Missouri River looking for strays that have got beyond the drift fences."

Alden nodded and looked at me from under his grizzled eyebrows.

"About the bills of sale: can you sign them for both the brands?" he asked.

"I think I can, but I'll call Mr. Warren at the bank to find out for sure. Everything we have is in both our names."

"What do you want to do with all the horses? They won't bring much at the stock ring. Better wait a little while till I hear of a farm sale, and we'll take 'em there. I hear the Army is looking for good saddle horses. Pardner and Devil and Blondie would bring a good price there. You plannin' to save back any of them?"

"Only Sammy. That was Jim's sister's horse. She should have him."

On and on we went with details. The heart within me was raw with searing emotions, but this clean cut must be made. I must get out of ranching. I knew this was the thing to do. I would go back to my profession as soon as another school year opened.

The following Wednesday night Alden drove up and knocked at the kitchen door. Stooping a little as he entered, he took off his hat and came over to the table where he seated himself.

"Well," he said as he took out the "making" for a cigarette, "we sold the first batch. Here are all the papers. You'd better go through these figures and weights with me. Made a killin' today. We ran the bidding up till we made the eastern buyers pay well for them. Got top prices for 'most everything." And he began pulling papers out of his leather jacket and piling them on the table. With a most inexperienced hand I began to check numbers, wishing I could put all this from me. Patiently Alden explained each item. Finally he leaned sideways and took from the hip pocket of his Levi's his bulging old billfold and began pulling out checks and laying them on the table before me.

"We'll finish up the job next week, Elsie. How about my putting the horses in my pasture in the valley until we sell them? And what do you think of keeping a couple of cows and calves for beef—keep 'em at my ranch? It'll give you plenty of meat. Want to save back one or two milk cows?"

I choked as I tried to answer. His kindness was so genuine that I felt comforted because Jim had such real friends—friends that continued true not only to him but also to me and the children.

Again the following week we checked and counted and added. The cattle were all sold except the few I would keep; the horses were taken care of for now.

Now came the agonizing experience of paying the debts, the mortgages, the loans on the stock. We had been married only six years. We had borrowed much money. My trip to the bank was traumatizing for me without Jim. My ignorance about finance was so complete.

"You can trust Mr. Warren," Jim had said so often. I did. I went to his office and paid and collected the notes and checked off in my mind how much money there would be left.

"What would you do with the money, Mr. Warren, if you were I?" I asked. "I know there's not too much of it, but it is a protection for the children."

His forehead wrinkled all the way up to his white hair as he thought before replying.

"There are many things I could suggest. But the safest place would be government bonds or postal savings. Postal savings pay only 2 percent, but it's so easy to get your money out of them when you need it. Let's see . . . there's a little over two thousand dollars here. Can you manage without this?"

I nodded and thanked him, not daring to say more. I checked my bank balance, drew out that sum, and headed for the post office, saying to myself, "It'll be a backlog. If anything happens that I need it, I can always get it quickly."

The next day I went into Bozeman to clear up details of the rented land. Alden was right. People were kind, especially right now, but their sympathy often unnerved me. I could take problems but not sympathy. Yet somewhere in the back of my mind I stored these thoughtful words and gestures. I sensed they would be as a fire to warm myself by in the lonely years ahead.

CHAPTER FOUR

Living on a ranch in the mountains we had had to move down into the valley each winter for feed for the cattle. Our place was high up in the foothills, the house located in a canyon, and the snow got very deep there. Before we were married, Jim had lived alone in the ranch house except for occasional cowboys to help him. It was a simple thing for him to go down to the valley, buy feed for the months of November to May—straw, hay, pasture, a place to feed the cattle—and find a home where the people would let him board. He moved the cattle down and lived near the feed grounds. All winter he would haul out the loads of hay or seed cake, keep the ice cut at the water holes, and enjoy the society of the close neighbors.

Having a family made it more difficult. After two rather unsuccessful years of moving us to a rented place for the winter, Jim decided to buy a bit of land in the valley and build a small log house. Off and on all that summer Jim and the cowboy who was then working for us cut trees, peeled them, and hauled them to the valley. On the corner which we bought an old fellow had a service station—just a tiny, one-room cabin and some red gasoline pumps. He wanted to return to Virginia, he said, and offered to sell us the cabin and the service station for a small amount. We bought it all.

Often, up at the ranch that summer, Beverly—who was a year old by then—would walk down past the shop where the saddle horses were shod and talk to Jim as he peeled the logs for our new home. Beverly played with old horseshoes and nails. Jim and I planned our house as he wielded his double-bitted ax, peeling off the bark from the native pine logs. We would have a two-room house to begin with. The construction of the building went slowly. In August Jim had to stop to round up cattle and sell the fat dry cows. In September he had riders to help him bring the cows and calves into the big corrals near the ranch house. The calves were taken from the cows, put into another pasture, later sold and shipped. In October the fat two-year-old steers were driven to Manhattan and loaded on the freight cars. By November the cattle had to be rounded up and moved to the valley for the winter feed.

The little log house in the valley had the windows and doors now and the cracks between the logs "pointed." The snow was getting deep in the canyon where the ranch house stood when Jim finally moved us to the little unfinished cabin beside the big red gasoline pumps. In the meantime I had added a pair of twins to our family. Five of us squeezed into the two rooms—a rather tight fit! All winter we worked on the inside of the house, building cupboards, papering, and painting.

In the spring we moved back to the ranch and hired some-one to care for the little service station. That summer Jim added another room to our house in the valley, and the winter following we were more comfortable. The summer before he died, he had added a big living room, a screened-in porch, and an office for the gas station.

All winter long the house was empty except for an oc-casional rider who happened in and spent the night there. It was an unwritten law of the ranch country that a house was left unlocked. Not once did we find that anything had been stolen. Often when we opened the doors in the spring we found several scribbled notes, written on the backs of calendar pages, such as this: "Thanks for the food and lodging. I found some potatoes and cabbages and canned meat in the root cellar and helped myself." One other part of that unwritten law was evident. The dishes that had been used had been carefully washed and dried and put away.

Now, having completed the details of giving the ranch back to the owner, from whom Jim had always rented it, I was leaving it permanently. Eunice and I packed everything, put the boxes in the back of the car, and brought load after load to the valley.

On the last trip, I went alone. The sun was just dropping behind the mountain as I drove up to the yard gate. I got out of the car and took the dusty path past the chicken house, on past the loading chute, through the first corral, past the cow barn, the horse barn, on through the big corral. Slowly I walked up the path toward the yard and opened the gate, noticing the familiar squeak of the hinges as the weight swung slowly down. As I went up the wooden walk I thought how many times that comforting gate squeak had told me Jim was home from a long ride.

In the house I moved from room to room, checking windows and looking for forgotten objects; then I went up the steep steps to the bedrooms upstairs. I opened each clothes closet door and glanced inside, made sure the windows were locked, and went back down to the living room, the dining room, the kitchen, and the back porch. I took from a wooden peg an unnoticed pair of spurs and a pair of Jim's chaps. Taking them with me I went out the back door, shutting it firmly, went down the wooden walk past the dining room windows where the climbing cucumber vines rustled dryly in the stir of air, through the protesting gate, and out to my waiting car.

For just a moment I turned and looked at the ranch house. It was here Jim had brought me as a bride. My eyes lifted to the head of the canyon and on up to the top of the mountain behind.

"I will lift up mine eyes unto the hills," I said softly as I got into the car and drove on down the road.

This chapter of my life was closed.

CHAPTER FIVE

For several months after Jim's death Eunice continued to work for me. She was a joy to have around the house. Her good humor was infectious, her comical remarks so catchy that I found myself imitating them. She'd say to one of the children, "Oh, go ahead; it'll do you good, besides helping you." As she stood at the sink washing dishes and one of the children asked her a question, she'd call back, "I don't know; can't tell from where I'm sittin'."

Watching her eat breakfast was a fascinating experience. Good-naturedly she took her turn at hopping up and down to help with the children, but gradually her own breakfast began to assume shape. First came a big bowl of cooked cereal; into this she would slide a soft fried egg, cutting it up carefully. Cream and sugar added to the top, she would mix thoroughly and begin to take generous spoonfuls. The first time I saw her make this mixture, I was sure she had absentmindedly put the egg into the cereal. I gasped audibly, but she said, "Never mind, Mis' Doig. I always say to my stomach, 'If you can mix things, so can I.' I like it this way—saves time in my eating."

Eunice liked music. She bought me several popular pieces when she went to town one day.

"You play a few pieces for me while I wash the dishes," she would say. "Play 'em good and loud, and I'll sing with you." I recognized it as a ruse to get me to rest, but I felt good inside when she did this.

A regular boyfriend came to see her on Saturday nights, took her to her home, then out on a date. He brought her back on Sunday night. I knew it was very late when she finally came into the house, almost morning, but the next day she was as gay and tireless as ever. She needed no more sleep than the swallows that wakened with the first light of dawn in the summer.

One Sunday night that winter, long after midnight, I heard the boyfriend's car drive up in front of the house and stop. I dropped off to sleep, then woke and heard the motor of the car running, idling.

It must be very cold and they're warming up with the heater of the car, I thought, and dozed off again. Waking again, I was aware that the car motor was still running. I looked at the clock. Twenty minutes until three. I began to get tense. On and on droned the motor. I began to think of the many stories I had heard of people's being asphyxiated by the fumes from the exhaust pouring into the car. This often occurred when the pipe had become stuffed full of snow. I thought of the snowy roads between Eunice's home and ours. Again I looked at the clock. Three o'clock. With a jerk I threw back the covers and bounced from my bed, pushed my feet into cold shoes, reached for my flashlight under my pillow, and hurried across the icy floor. Out the kitchen door I went, forgetting to grab a coat. There sat the car, its motor idling away. I flashed my light into the car. I could see two bodies crumpled over. I ran to the car and yanked open the front door nearest me. Eunice tumbled against me and her boyfriend fell against her—both tumbling almost out of the car. I yelled my astonishment as I pushed against their bodies to keep them from falling to the ground. Suddenly they began to pull themselves up, opened their eyes, and grinned sleepily.

"I'm sorry," I apologized confusedly, and mumbled incoherently something about thinking they were dead.

"Guess we went to sleep," Eunice said, still a bit confused.

Turning off my flashlight, I made an embarrassed exit and hurried back to my warm bed, resolving never to let my fears fool my mind again.

But I have eaten every resolution I have ever made, and this was no exception. About a month later I had to let Eunice go. I was making so very little money with the service station now that it was winter and the ranchers were not traveling out to town that I could not afford to keep her. Besides, I had become accustomed to taking care of the babies and felt that I could manage alone. I had to learn— no use putting it off any longer.

All my life I had been afraid to be alone. The craziest things worried me. I began to notice that there was a rash of service station holdups, especially those that were in out-of-the-way places, such as mine was. I scanned every newspaper for these items. My service station office was a room of the house, a room projected out front, intended for a bedroom eventually. Each night I carefully locked the door of the service station room, then locked the door that led into the living room of the house. But the least sound in that part of the house at night sent chills up my spine. Often I would grab my flashlight and investigate.

One night about midnight I awoke suddenly. I thought I had heard a car drive up in front of the station and stop. I awaited a honking of the horn, a call, or a pounding on the door. Out in the country as our station was, we had frequently served customers at night in emergencies. But as I lay listening there was complete silence. If you've never been in the country, far away from cities and highways, you don't know how deep a silence can be. Lying tensely in bed I waited. Still no sound! Drops of sweat formed on my forehead and I brushed them off with the sleeve of my nightgown. It was so quiet . . . only the gentle breathing of the children in their beds and baskets. . . . I could stand it no longer. I jumped from the bed and stepped into my shoes, fumbling for the flashlight, stumbling through the house with no light so that I would not wake the babies.

As I approached the kitchen door, I stopped and listened again. My ear drums pounded and hurt with the intensity of my listening. I opened the door and snapped on the big floodlight that illuminated the whole acre surrounding the house. There in front of the house squatted the two big gas pumps, looking like sentinels with their black shadows stretching away from them. I strained my eyes to look in each direction.

Just east of the house, about thirty yards across the road, was a deep gravel pit. Could the car have driven down into the pit? I was impelled by my fear to go to see. I flashed my light down into the depths of the pit. Nothing there!

Perhaps the car had stopped, let someone off, and then gone on. There might be someone hiding somewhere. A shed-like building stood a few yards to the north of the house, partly in shadows. Going back into the house, I came out with the keys and unlocked the shed. I flashed my light into the dirty, floorless room. Barrels of oil were balanced horizontally on wooden horses. Into every corner of the building I looked, squatting to peer under the barrels whose wooden spigots made strange shadows on the dirt floor. Satisfied at last that there was no one hiding there, I locked the shed and slowly walked around the grounds.

Finally exhausted from the futile search, I went back to bed. It was a long time before I slept. But never again did I have that unconquerable fear that someone might hurt me. Somehow this traumatizing experience had washed me clean of the unreasonable fear of danger from an unknown source.

CHAPTER SIX

The weather continued cold through November. We were shut in the house most of the time. One day my sister Irene and her fiance Harry drove into the yard. Their faces glowed with happiness as they got out of their car.

"It's Aunt Irene and Kelly," I called to the children. Beverly dropped her toys, ran to open the door, and stood there expectantly. Kelly scooped her up into his arms as Irene stooped to let the older twins hug her.

"Elsie," she said over Margie's and Marilyn's heads, "we're going to be married next week at Jacobs' house. We decided not to put it off longer. You understand, don't you?"

I nodded.

"We will have a private wedding, just a few couples, no fuss. Now, will you sing for us?"

"Oh, I can't." It wasn't modesty. I just knew that I could not do this. "You have friends who are good soloists who will do this for you."

"Then we won't have any solo at all," Harry said firmly.

We discussed it for a while, but Harry was adamant. He won. When they left I had promised; the song and accompanist had been chosen. The whole week long I alternately made up excuses for not doing it and then shamed myself into some backbone. Suppose I broke down and began to cry. I had not yet gained control of my emotions, and music—especially choral music—made me cry so easily. It would spoil all the gaiety of the wedding if I started dripping tears.

My uncle, a missionary, came to Bozeman to perform the ceremony. He drove out to my house to stay with me.

His matter-of-factness gave me courage. Irene had bought a lovely pink dress for Beverly to wear as flower girl. There were little embroidered figures around the skirt. Irene's gown was ivory taffeta. Her expressive brown eyes shone with emotion as she modeled the gown for me when I went into town to get supplies for the station and stopped in to see her for a few minutes. She laughed as she talked of her fiance.

"You should see Harry. He's so scared that he gets pasty white when we even talk of the wedding." Together we enjoyed the thought of Kelly's discomfiture.

The evening of the wedding came. The children, eager for excitement, jiggled as I buttoned dresses and combed hair. On the tiny twins in their baskets I put sleeping gowns. They would not waken, I hoped.

Starting the car early, I let the motor run to warm the car with the heater. Several trips back and forth I made from the house to the car, putting the baskets in the back seat, one end of each resting on a stump of log between the seats as Jim had taught me to do. Beverly sat between the baskets to watch the babies and keep them warmly covered. Margie and Marilyn, snug in their snowsuits, climbed onto the front seat beside me.

As I drove toward town an old nagging fear entered my mind. If I should get stalled with the car what could I do? I couldn't walk for help and leave the children. I could not carry them all. These thoughts had kept me at home with the children day after day for two months. But I drove carefully and began to think of seeing people, of going some place, of the old associations.

When we arrived in Bozeman, I stopped before the Jacobs home. In a moment two people came running from the house to my car to help me carry the children. We put the baskets with the sleeping babies in the back bedroom. So busy was I with the children that I had not thought of the solo I was to sing. Now my hands began to get cold, and my knees felt as if there were no strength in the joints. But when I stood up to sing, I imagined Jim to be sitting across the room, right in front of the radio. I sang to him, "When the dawn flames in the sky, I love. . . ." I was not afraid. In a few minutes the service was over.

In the confusion of the congratulations of the bride and groom, I was able to slip unnoticed from the room. I went to look at the babies. They were sleeping quietly. Suddenly the emotions I had pushed off so long swept over me, and I sobbed until I was shaking. Then I felt an arm around me. Mrs. Hansen, my former eighth-grade teacher, said in my ear, "It's all right, Elsie; we understand. You can cry if you need to."

But in a few minutes I did not need to cry anymore. I was all right now. I followed her into the kitchen where she gave me an ice-cream dipper and put me to work. And I dipped until my hands became steady and I could look up and smile at the happy couple.

One more experience had given me strength to face other experiences in the future.

CHAPTER SEVEN

"You can't keep them all, my dear," my mother had said after Jim's funeral. "It's impossible. Think of them. You're selfish to want to keep them. Think how much they could have if your brother adopted some of them."

I did think. Five children! How could I expect to support and care for them alone? I had very little money. One brother had written, "We'll take any of them. We have none of our own."

I knew that he would give them a good home. He was a doctor; his wife had been teaching home economics in the college before they were married. I liked them both very much.

But it is hard for a mother to give up one of her children. It is difficult for the mind to control the emotions. Besides, which would I let go—to be adopted—which one? At night I looked them over when they were asleep as I walked from room to room and tried to convince myself. Not Beverly, my oldest, her father's pride. Nor Margie and Marilyn, the twins who were two years old. It couldn't be Jimmy, my only son, the exact replica of his father. It would have to be Joan, his little twin sister—Joan, the tiny, dimpled, curly-headed baby whose happy smile made us glad. No, we did not need her. She was really unnecessary. We had three girls already. She was the smallest, the youngest. A premature baby, still in her basket—surely it would be easier to give her up than any one of the others.

But the thought tore at my heart. Selfish? Perhaps I was. Was it selfish to want to keep one's own children? I suppose so, for I could not give them the temporal things that my brother could. His home was beautiful. His income was that of a successful man of his profession. Always he and his wife had wanted a baby of their own. His wife would be such a good mother to my little Joan.

And so I argued in my mind, convincing myself that this was the best thing to do.

Then came a letter from my brother saying that they thought it would be easier if the baby were a few months older. Besides, they could not come to Montana right then. I felt as if I had been given a temporary reprieve from a sentence.

But each night for several months I seemed to go through the process of giving her up. She wouldn't miss us, surely, but we would miss her.

The winter was bitter cold as Montana winters often are. Except for rare occasions we were alone—the children and I. Often I longed for adult companionship, but much of the time I was too busy or too tired to have time to think of myself.

On Christmas Day we went to the Jacobs home for dinner. Irene and Harry were there, the Hansens too. The children were given presents, were petted and admired, held on laps. I felt relaxed. Reluctantly, I took my family back to our little log cabin in the country, starting before dark because of the snowy roads.

The next morning Beverly's face was flushed. She coughed hoarsely. Taking her temperature that evening, I found it to be 104°. Sponge baths lowered it a bit. The other children were fretful. With so much flu around us, I could hardly expect to escape entirely, but they'd been so very healthy.

By Tuesday morning all five were ill. The lowest temperature was 102°. At my telephone call, the doctor started the thirty-mile drive on snowy roads. Although there was much to do I found time passing slowly as I waited. An hour or so later his car appeared and then pushed its nose against our little house before it stopped. He smiled at me quietly as he entered the kitchen.

Saying very little he went from one child to the next, deftly taking temperatures, noting pulses. When he raised his head after examining Joan, he spoke tersely, "Better put her in the hospital. Bronchial pneumonia. You have your hands full taking care of the others."

"When, doctor?" I was determined to seem as calm as the doctor was, but little butterflies were beating their wings inside my abdomen, for this was the first grave situation I had faced since the children's father had died.

"As soon as you can get her there," came his answer. "I'll make the arrangements at the hospital. Call me as soon as you get there."

He left a few sulfa pills, wrote a prescription, gave me some more instructions, and was gone in a whirl of snow. I called a neighbor and persuaded her oldest daughter to come help me for a few days.

By evening the sulfa had lowered the temperatures of the other children, but Joan's cough left her choking for breath, and I could not hear her cry because of the hoarseness. The phlegm almost filled her throat; I had to take it out by running my little finger down the inside of her mouth to her throat.

I must do something. The neighbor girl could take care of the other children while I made the trip to the hospital with Joan. Starting the car with the temperature twenty degrees below zero was another difficult task. But the car was my friend—it understood a crisis.

Putting Joan in her warm little "bunny-suit" and zipping it to her chin took only a few moments. Her basket would be necessary for her, I decided. As I gave last-minute instructions to the girl about the care of the children, I was getting into my coat, tying a scarf about my head, adding mittens, overshoes. My own cough was worse. I had had little sleep the last week.

On the way to the hospital, I rested as I drove. Soft snowflakes began to fall as I neared town. "Be dark soon," I warned myself. "Must hurry back home."

The nurses were kind to Joan. Several remembered when she was born there, just six months before. "Leave her basket here. We may use it," they suggested. "She's so tiny for a bed. We'll put her in a ward, Room 105, but she'll have to have special nurses."

By that time the doctor had arrived. He had X rays taken of the baby's chest and neck. The nurses led me into the darkroom to see the results.

"It is pneumonia. Look at those bronchial tubes," the doctor muttered.

Another doctor had come in. He went close to the lighted plates. "Bad case!" he said. "She'll never completely outgrow it. Even when she's grown, she'll have to guard her throat." His speech was crisp and succinct but not unsympathetic. He was an older doctor whom I had known for years.

"Never outgrow it!" The words cut into my mind. They hurt. I must warn my brother of this. Someone else, not I, would be caring for her soon.

As I left the darkroom, a nurse met me in the hall.

"Your special nurse has arrived. Do you want to talk to her before you go?"

The "special" was bending over Joan's basket as I entered the ward. She looked up. "Oh, Mrs. Doig, it's your baby. I didn't know." Her face and her voice were filled with solicitude. It was Miss Ferris, the nurse who had been with my husband when he died.

"Yes, this is one of my younger twins. But I'll not worry about Joan since I know you're on the case, and I'll telephone every day."

Relieved, I patted Joan and said good-bye.

The keen, sharp cold felt good to me as I hurried down the front steps of the hospital. I breathed deeply, gaining strength from the invigorating air. The snow had quit falling, and the stars were out. As I drove, I tried not to let my anxiety about the other children hurry my driving. The beauty of the night was restful. Bright moonlight pictured the mountains clearly. Majestic peaks, blanketed with deep, quiet snow, pushed their shoulders into a sky filled with stars. With David of old, I again murmured: "I will lift up mine eyes unto the hills from whence cometh my help. . . ." The thought fortified me for the long ride home and carried me into the house.

Quietly the neighbor girl spoke from the bedroom.

"They're better. All asleep. Jimmy's had his nine o'clock bottle. Coming to bed?"

The next three days the children at home improved gradually. Twice a day I called for news of Joan, but the hospital would give me no definite information.

"Condition about the same," was the usual answer.

Friday morning the idea that I must hurry to the hospital obsessed me. By noon I was on my way. It was difficult to keep my foot pressure light on the accelerator. I wanted to go faster and faster. At last I pulled up at the hospital, covered the car hood with a blanket, and ran up the steps and into the big building. My doctor met me in the hall.

"I was just going to call you, Mrs. Doig," he said. "Joan is very low. Her temperature can't be held below 105°.

White count very high. Won't take any nourishment nor water. She can't live if this goes on."

As he talked I was walking toward Joan's room, the doctor with me. Nearing the ward I recognized my baby's weak crying. I slipped off my coat as I entered the room, smiled at the nurse who was trying to coax Joan to drink a bottle of milk. I took the baby in my arms and began to hum an old lullaby. Joan settled against my breast for a few minutes.

"Has she been crying long?" I whispered to the nurse over the baby's head.

"Almost all the time," she answered.

Joan stirred and began to cry again. I resumed my humming as I picked up the bottle from the stand by the bed. Again she quieted as I sang. Gently I put the nipple against her mouth. At first she refused it, but after a little coaxing, she opened her mouth and began to take the milk hungrily. Fascinated, the nurse and the doctor stood near and watched. Then the doctor spoke.

"I wouldn't have believed it. A baby six months old homesick. You stay with her, Mrs. Doig. Don't let anyone tell you to leave. It is the only medicine that can make her well." And nodding to the nurse, he left the ward.

"I'll get a rocking chair for you," the nurse offered.

I watched the milk disappear from the bottle—two ounces, four ounces. I wiggled the nipple in her mouth. Sleepily she emptied the bottle. I talked softly to the nurse. She asked about the other children.

"Don't you want to try to lay her down?" she suggested at last.

Slowly I eased the sleeping baby onto the little bed and stretched my arms. But in an instant that fretful, weak cry came again. Restlessly she moved and cried. I took her in my arms again, spoke to her soothingly. After a few sobs she was quiet. For hours I held her as she slept. Often she woke and cried but always quieted when she was aware that I was holding her. Every three hours I gave her a bottle of milk. The special nurse had gone off duty. Lights had been turned low. Only now and then the rubber-heeled footsteps of a hurrying nurse sounded in the hall.

About midnight Joan was quiet for so long that I tried again to lay her in the bed. This time she did not stir as I gently covered her and tiptoed from the room, taking my coat with me. Catching a nurse in the hall, I explained.

"I'm going to curl up on the davenport in the waiting room and sleep a while. Wake me if she stirs."

"I will, Mrs. Doig. Your eyes look so heavy. Do sleep." She put her hand on my shoulder as she passed.

How kind the nurses are, I thought as I lay on the davenport. Caring for children had taught me to relax whenever I could. Almost instantly I was asleep.

A gentle pressure on my shoulder roused me. Penetrating my consciousness was a quiet voice.

"She's crying again. Want to come?"

I looked at my watch—four o'clock—and then hurried to my feet. The nurse went before me down the dimly lighted hall to the ward. Joan's wailing cry reached us before we neared the door. Hastily I picked her up and quieted her. How light she was! But her little body seemed not quite so hot as it had been in the afternoon and evening. For hours I held her, laying her down once in a while when I went outside to walk for a few minutes.

Later in the morning I telephoned home. The slow, steady voice of the neighbor girl reassured me that the children were better.

For longer periods Joan slept. Her temperature dropped

gradually to normal—to below normal—to ninety-six degrees. About four o'clock in the afternoon she became very quiet. Her pulse could hardly be counted; her breathing, almost undetectable. I watched her closely. At last I went to the telephone and called the doctor.

"She's so very quiet. She has reached the crisis, I believe. Can you come tell me whether she'll live or not? I must know," I told him.

As I waited for him, I leaned against the doorcasing and began to pray in my heart, "Dear God, don't let her die. Don't ask me to give her up. I know that we don't need another child, but I can't go home and tell the children that she's dead. I told them of their father's death just three months ago. Please don't make me carry another message like that. It would break their hearts. They love her so. She's part of us. . . ."

The doctor entered the room quietly, bent over the baby, listened with his stethoscope, talked to the nurse on duty. At last he turned to me.

"She's going to get well, I think, Mrs. Doig. Stay with her today and tonight, and you can take her home tomorrow."

I turned aside so that the doctor would not see my tears and said huskily, "Thank you, doctor." It was all I could say.

But silently I was saying, "Thank you, God. We'll keep her. She needs us, and we need her."

Never again did I consider letting one of my children be adopted.

CHAPTER EIGHT

No one ever had better neighbors than we did. Some of them stopped to see us almost every day. Our house stood on the corner of the Dry Creek crossroads. Just across from us was the little white church where I often played for services. Down the road west a half mile was the schoolhouse. Almost everyone went past our house on the way to town—whether it was to Belgrade, Manhattan, or Bozeman. To provide a little income, I continued to operate the service station, to sell candy and gum and kerosene and other articles. Most of our neighbors bought their gasoline from us. Eunice and I took turns running out to the pumps when a car stopped as long as she was with me.

Each morning that winter I bought a gallon of milk from the neighbors just north of us, paying them a nominal sum. Usually they managed to send it to me rather than have me walk to their home for it.

The Crowalls, who lived south of us, took care of the few head of cattle I had not sold and would not let me pay them for this. In the spring, the two cows had calves. Alden put both calves on one cow and brought the other cow to the pasture just across the road from our house. Mornings and evenings, equipped with the three-legged milking stool and a bucket, I walked out into the pasture and by shaking a pan of ground oats coaxed the cow to come to me. As she ate the feed, I sat on the stool, the milk pail between my knees, and hurriedly milked her. If she finished before I did, I followed her around the pasture, trying to complete the stripping. I had brought the cream separator down from the ranch. Once a day I separated the milk to have cream for butter and skimmed milk for cottage cheese. The remainder of the milk we drank.

In November Alden had one of my two-year-old steers butchered, taken to Belgrade, the meat cut up and wrapped and put in my locker at the freezing plant there. When I went to town for supplies, I would bring home several packages of the beef.

Often my neighbors brought me a dressed hen, a side of pork, some fresh sausage, or—if someone had been hunting— a few packages of fresh venison or elk. All of this, added to my hundreds of jars of canned vegetables and fruit, made our diet completely balanced.

To the south and east of us lived the Milestons. John tried to persuade me not to sell the cattle when I left the ranch. "I'll take care of them for you," he offered. "Won't cost you anything but the feed." But I could not accept the offer. It would mean complications, obligations, and involvements that I knew I could not face.

Often that winter the Milestons stopped to see me and the children. One evening they drove up before the house. Mrs. Mileston got out of the car, and her husband went on down the road toward the west. When I opened the door in answer to her knocking, she said, "Elsie, I'm going to visit with you while John is at the schoolhouse for a meeting. Go on with your putting the children to bed. I'll follow you about."

She took off her hat and coat and came into the bedroom where I was undressing the older twins.

"Beverly," she said, "let me unbutton those hard ones." And she reached out to help the little girl.

We talked of the children, of their little happenings, as we got them ready for their beds. In the living room later, Mrs. Mileston said suddenly, "Elsie, John said I should tell you of my early life. We never talk of it. Don't mind me if I get all teary."

She began with her first marriage at eighteen, her husband's drowning that winter in the river before the baby was born, her lonely vigil up and down the riverbank, looking for the body of her husband. She told of that year of grief, and then of John's understanding and love, of his marrying her, and of the four children born subsequently.

Fascinatedly I listened. Although I had known this family for years, I had never suspected that the oldest girl was not John's.

"I am telling you this," Mrs. Mileston ended, "so you will know that we do know something of your experience this year. We think we understand."

And then we talked of other things, but the bond between us was closer.

But all receiving and no giving distorts one's personality. It was difficult for me to reciprocate the many kindnesses of my neighbors. One thing I could do, however insignificant it seemed to me: I could play the wheezy old pump organ in the little community church across the road. Sunday school was held in the afternoon—no conflict with morning attendance at my own church in Bozeman, whenever I could manage to go there. Special services for our community were usually set for the evening.

The Easter exercises that year scared me. I could not yet face such things as "resurrection" and "life after death" without emotional agony. I knew I must discipline myself, learn to look straight at these tenets of religion, beliefs that were a basic part of my life.

Much disturbed as I played for the Easter service that evening, I dropped my head, low enough so that the congregation could not see my face over the organ. With the closing of the program, I moved quickly through the crowd, out of the church, across the road, and into the seclusion of my kitchen. Closing the door, I leaned weakly against the casing and sobbed convulsively for a few minutes. Suddenly the door opened. I didn't even look up as I struggled to stop crying.

"Elsie." It was Mrs. Nebrun's voice. I never knew there could be so much compassion in a voice. "We were afraid you would do this. They sent me over to . . . to . . . to comfort you."

A few weeks later I found myself analyzing my thoughts. "The trouble with me is," I said to the empty kitchen, as I put coal in the stove for the night and closed the drafts, "that I can't get out of myself. I think too much about *me*. I must do something for someone, forget myself."

For a while I stood there musing, then went to bed with this still on my mind. By morning I had conceived a solution—rather an absurd one, I knew, but I would try it. Living in Bozeman was Mrs. Hansen, my former grade school teacher and her husband, who owned and operated a little corner grocery store. Working long hours in their business, they ate hastily prepared meals of "store food." I would take them some homemade bread and cottage cheese, something they did not have.

With my mind on something besides myself, my children, and my problems, I worked with a light heart the next day, kneading the dough and baking it, carefully heating the sour milk until the curds rolled gently between my fingers, draining off the whey, rinsing the cheese again and again, pouring on the rich cream. On my regular trip to town for supplies for the station the next day, I took with me the strange gifts to the home of the Hansens, an apartment in the back of the store.

"I'm bringing these things to you, Mrs. Hansen," I said as I held out the brown paper sacks, "not because you need to have them but because I need to give them. I hope you'll understand."

I stood looking at her belligerently, daring her to laugh or say anything negative. She smiled, put her arms around me, and shook me gently as she said, "I do, Elsie; I understand."

CHAPTER NINE

When we were adding a living room to the little log house in the valley, we had begun to plan for water for our home. During the two winters that we had spent there, Jim had hauled water for us. This was most inconvenient, especially with the addition of babies. So Jim had had a well drilled under the foundation, in the cellar beneath the living room, the casing and pipe put in, and an electric pump and a tank installed there. A pipe led to the kitchen—a faucet on it, preparatory for the sink we planned to have later. Running water—what a luxury! By this time we had been able to connect with the power lines in the valley and also had electricity.

In February of our first year without Jim, the pump began to wheeze and bring up only small quantities of water and the last of that was muddy, especially when I would run enough to fill a tub to heat for washing. I thought there must be something wrong with the pump. Shorty Benson came to look at it for me. He took it all apart and examined the valves. Together we pulled up all the pipe, looked at everything, and put it back as it had been.

"I can't find anything wrong," he said. "Must be the electric motor. Take it back to the store where you bought it. Take the pump too."

"I have no idea where Jim got them." I said.

"Well, find any store that handles Briggs-Stratton motors, and you can get them repaired. They carry a good guarantee, I'm sure, and you haven't had them a year yet." He disconnected the pump and motor and put them in the trunk of my car.

"Sorry I couldn't really help you," he said as I tried to thank him.

The next morning I drove to Bozeman, found a hardware store that sold Briggs-Stratton motors, and persuaded a service man to help me unload my machinery at the back door. Helplessly I watched him examine the motor and pump. I waited for hours. About noon he beckoned to me. "We'll put them back into your car. Nothing wrong that I can see. That'll be twenty-two dollars," he said as he slammed the trunk lid.

I must have gasped audibly, for he quickly added, "Labor, you see."

I paid him and drove home, shaking my head. Another S.O.S. call to Shorty, who came to help me put it all back together down in the basement. When he turned on the switch the pump sucked up a bit of muddy water, wheezed, and then gave forth nothing. I turned off the electricity and we went up the steps, discouraged.

For several weeks I had been carrying all the water for our house from the Nisbets' pump, a quarter of a mile away. It took many gallons for the whole family, especially with the babies in diapers. I took two five-gallon milk cans, put them in Beverly's little wagon, carried a three-gallon bucket in one hand, and pulled the wagon with the other. Beverly and the older twins usually went with me. Every day, at least once, we went after water. Sometimes—especially on washdays—we went several times. It was exhausting. For weeks this continued.

But Shorty was still trying to solve my problem. One day he stopped at the house, accompanied by another neighbor. Both men carried spades.

"We think we've stumbled onto a solution," Shorty said. "You know how dry it's been this year; well, the water level has been dropping everywhere in the valley. Dry Creek is running only a small stream. Wells are low."

He waited for me to say something. I nodded my head, trying to think along with him.

"Now, if we go down about four—maybe five—feet and set the motor and pump down that far, I'll bet you'll have water."

I led the way to the steps that went to the basement. The two men lowered their spades from their shoulders and began to dig—all around the pump. Shorty disconnected the motor, propped it and the pump on some two-by-fours, and went on digging.

Eunice and I carried buckets of dirt up the steps and out into the yard. In a few hours the men had a hole deep enough and large enough that they could lower the pump and the motor and make them all secure about four feet below the level of the dirt floor.

"Keep your fingers crossed," Shorty said over his shoulder. "We're gonna' try the pump."

He flipped on the switch. The motor hummed and the pump began to wheeze, then we could hear water gurgling as it started to fill the tank.

"Go up and turn on a faucet," he called to me.

Up the steps I ran and into the kitchen. Out of the faucet came water—very muddy at first, then gradually clearer.

"How's it coming?" Shorty yelled from down in the cellar.

"Water," I called. "Still dirty, but it's water."

"Let it run—it'll take a long time to clear."

As I went back down the steps, the men looked at me and grinned and began to carry out the remainder of the dirt and clean up the basement.

"I can do the rest," I told them. In the best way I could

I thanked these neighbors of mine. I knew they would not accept money.

"It's okay now. I can sleep better tonight," Shorty said as he and the other man started to drive away.

I rubbed my aching muscles and said, "Me too."

Hurrying into the house, I turned off the faucet. What a blessing water is, I thought, as I looked into the eyes of the three little girls who waited to be told all about it.

CHAPTER TEN

It was spring before an elder visited our church in Bozeman. My uncle, Lester Wildermuth, missionary to our area, wrote that he was coming to see us. As I read the letter, I said aloud, "Oh, I can have the babies blessed."

Margie and Marilyn looked up from their tea party.

"What is that, Mama?" Margie usually spoke first.

"Oh, you know," Beverly explained with her four-year-old wisdom. "Don't you remember about Jesus blessing the little children? It's like that, isn't it, Mother?"

I nodded.

"Was I blessed?" Marilyn wanted to know.

"Of course," I reminisced. "Daddy held Margie, and I held you."

"How old was I then?" Beverly asked. "I can't remember, can I?"

"No, you weren't even two years old yet." I laid the letter in my lap. "Now, let's see. We must make plans."

The little girls left their table, pulling their red chairs close to where I sat.

"What shall we have them wear?" I pondered. "Oh, I'd like a special song. How can we manage that?"

No one answered me.

"I know. You three can sing one verse of 'Suffer Little Children.' How about that?"

We went to the piano, and I opened the hymnal and began to play the music of the song.

"You know some of the words, don't you? We'll sing just the first verse."

By rote we learned the words, a line at a time. They

already knew the melody. All week we continued to sing the song—while I was washing dishes . . . when I was cooking supper . . . whatever I was doing, we sang.

Saturday afternoon I drove to Bozeman to meet Uncle Lester as he came into town on the train. I told him of our plans for him to bless the babies; he nodded and talked of their names.

Sunday morning was a busy time. Up early, we began to get ready as soon as our cereal was eaten and the dishes were washed. Except for Joan's dress and Jim's rompers, they were soon ready and in their baskets. Uncle Lester supervised their taking their bottles of milk, sitting between the baskets, talking to the babies all the while.

"Mother, will you reach my dress for me, the pink one Auntie Irene got me for her wedding?" Beverly stood on tiptoe by the curtained-off corner that we called our clothes closet.

I handed her the dress, took the blue dresses to Margie and Marilyn, and slipped one over each head, smoothing down the silky fine hair I had put on curlers very early that morning.

"Button me up, Mother."

"Go to Uncle Lester, Beverly. He likes to help little girls," I said as my fingers pushed buttons through holes.

Loading everyone and everything into the car took many trips back and forth from the house. I glanced at the kitchen clock as I closed the dampers on the cookstove, peeked into the oven to look at the roast, and then shut the kitchen door after me, pulling on my coat as I walked to the car.

"Just nine o'clock, Uncle Les," I said, starting the motor. "We'll be there in plenty of time. Sunday school doesn't begin until ten."

59

We talked as we drove—I had so many things to tell him. He was interested. Not often did I have an opportunity to talk to someone who was really concerned about all the details of my family.

At the church the same process occurred in reverse as we transferred baskets and sleeping babies. Sunday school was almost over when Jimmy and Joan awoke.

At the beginning of the next service, I propped Jim in one corner of a front pew with Joan beside him. The older twins and Beverly and I awaited expectantly the ending of the opening prayer. With the little girls close by I went to the piano and played a few measures of the song. Turning my face toward them I mouthed the words as they sang softly, " 'Suffer little children,' Jesus said, as he placed a blessing on each head. . . ." As she sang, Marilyn looked down at her dress and twisted her skirt in her hands, but Margie and Beverly looked directly at me and remembered each word.

The last syllables finished, we returned to the front pew where I stooped to pick up Jimmy and take him to Uncle Lester for the blessing. I wasn't aware of the words of the prayer, for I was talking to the Lord, asking His help. Then came a transfer of babies. On Joan's head the soft hair curled in natural ringlets. Her tiny face with its delicate contours, her quick smile of response to Uncle Lester's smile as he took her in his arms, brought a murmur from the audience.

Again I bowed my head and thanked God that I had decided to keep this baby girl, and asked His reassurance that I had done what was best for her and the other children.

CHAPTER ELEVEN

Always, after selling the cattle and giving up the ranch, in my mind there was the thought of the necessity of going back to teaching school as a support for my family. Before I was married and for a year after, I had been a "school-puncher"—as the cowboys called me—in a rural school. In the summer vacations I had attended college, in this way getting my degree.

Now my certificate had to be renewed. To do this I would have to have eight new college credits. Soon after Christmas I began two correspondence courses of four credits each from the University of Montana. Sandwiching in the hours of study for these courses was another problem. I finally figured out a system.

After Jim's accident, I could no longer nurse the babies. Their prematureness had given them delicate constitutions. Immediately after I had put them on bottles they began to have colic. Often at night they cried for hours. So I would prop one on the davenport, rock the other one in one arm— switching babies now and then—and study. My neighbors on the north said they could set their clocks by my lights at night—usually from two to four o'clock—they said. When the babies became quieter and I was exhausted, I would put them in their baskets and go to bed, to dream of the Irish kings and heroes that I had been reading about in the literature course I was taking.

We progressed. The lessons were sent in somewhat ir-regularly, but by summer I knew I could renew my certifi-cate. I began to ask around about teaching positions. The trustees of the Dry Creek School offered me a position there.

However, I could not find anyone who would be a full-time housekeeper if I continued to live in the country. So I went to the neighboring towns to apply. I made an appointment with the superintendent of schools in Manhattan. He looked at me with skepticism when I made my personal application.

"You mean you have five small children and still expect to . . . to . . . ?" He sounded incredulous.

"I'll have a housekeeeper. I can make good. I know I can—I must. I'll be a better teacher because of my children. If I fail, I'll fail them."

Unconvinced, he shook his head and dismissed me with a muttered, "I'll think it over." His tone was not convincing.

This was the summer of 1941. Teaching jobs were not easy to get. The aftermath of the depression was still evident in our part of the country. But on the school board was a rancher friend of Jim's. I talked to him, and I am sure he "twisted the superintendent's arm," as he suggested he might. Within a month I was hired to teach second grade and music in the lower grades. Of course I wanted to teach in high school—that was what I had been studying for all these years—but I was thankful for an opportunity to teach anything, anywhere.

I began to look for a house to rent in Manhattan. I found three vacant ones. The first one appealed to me. It was clean and roomy, near the schoolhouse.

"I like it," I told the owner. "How much a month did you say the rent is?"

"Let's see, I've been getting—say, wait a minute!" She stopped short. "Do you have any children?"

"Oh, yes," I said eagerly, expecting sympathy.

"How many?"

"Five, but they're just little ones."

"I can't rent to you. Don't want anyone with five children tearing my house down."

"But they're only babies. The oldest one is four years old."

She shook her head and started to go back into her house. I was so surprised that I didn't even argue with her.

At the next house almost the same thing happened, and also at the third. I began to get panicky. I had to have a place to live, and no one would rent me a house.

As I began to cudgel my brain for an idea, "Why not buy one?" kept coming to my mind. Again I drove to Manhattan to inquire. Yes, there was one large old house for sale. I found the owner on his farm south of town. He offered me the key to the house, and I went back to town, found the house, and unlocked the front door. Slowly I walked through the living room, pausing to look out the front window at a big maple tree in the front yard—"Good branches for a swing for the children," I said to myself— then the dining room, the kitchen, the hall and stairs, the bedrooms on the second floor.

Later I went out into the backyard where a small barn stood. The pleasant odor of dry hay greeted me as I opened the door and climbed the steep, dusty stairs to the hayloft. "A good place for play on rainy days," my mind recorded, as I kicked at the piles of musty hay and peered down the openings to the mangers below.

The owner had already given me the price—exactly the amount that I had in postal savings. I went home to ponder it over. The next day I drew my money out of the post office, went to the owner, and then to the bank to complete the deal of buying the house. The children were with me, waiting in the car in Beverly's charge until I came back out of the bank. We drove to look at the "new" house.

With one twin baby on each hip and the other three

children close to my skirts, I took them through the house and barn, explaining all the "fun" we were going to have this winter. Upstairs we picked out the bedroom for Margie and Marilyn and Beverly, and decided where each bed would stand. We talked about where Jim and Joan's little beds would be put in my bedroom. We inspected the bathroom—the first one we had ever had—talking about how much fun it would be to get into a big tub and have lots of water.

Downstairs we explored the bedroom for our housekeeper. Often I had to stop and put Jim and Joan on the floor to rest my tired arms. But I wanted them to become acquainted with the house, to take away the strangeness. This must be a family experience, one the children understood and were prepared for. We went home, chattering happily together.

The next thing to be considered was the little service station. This problem solved itself so quickly that I felt the solution just fell into my lap. A young couple who had been living in Crowalls' bunkhouse were glad of the opportunity to take over the small business. The fellow continued to work at the Crowall ranch while his wife tended the station.

Now there was only the problem of moving and getting settled before school began. I was scared—really panicky—of the changes I was making, but I knew that I had considered each angle. Teaching was a good occupation for me for the future. In a few years the children would be in school. We would have our vacations at the same time. In the summers I could make their clothes and raise a garden. We would be together as much as we could.

The first day of school was a traumatizing experience for me. The children had hardly become acquainted with the new housekeeper. The house still was not really home. When I left for school that morning, they did not cry, but I did—as soon as I was out of sight. The three older ones followed me to the edge of our lot, stood there waving at me, their eyes sober and intense. I walked slowly down the tree-shaded street, looking back now and then to the spot of color made by their dresses. I felt that I was deserting them, that somehow I had betrayed a trust. But deep down inside me I knew that this was the best thing I could do.

The days in the classroom were good. I liked the challenge of helping children learn. Although primary grades were not my choice I was glad to have a job, an income. I found companionship among the teachers. They were a good crew, conscientious, hard-working, willing to share ideas, eager to help me get adjusted. The hours in school went by rapidly.

After the students had gone home for the evening and I had prepared my work for the next day, I would hurry home to find the three little girls waiting, sitting on an old stump near the edge of our lawn. Together we would go into the house where I would scoop up Jim and Joan from the floor. Then sitting in the big rocking chair, with them in my lap, with Margie and Marilyn in their little chairs beside me and Beverly at my feet, I would let them absorb me, their only parent. I told them the stories I had read to the students that day. Often I taught them the little songs the first and second graders enjoyed singing. For an hour at least we sat together. Sometimes I would go to the piano and play the pieces I had been teaching in the rhythm band. Slowly their loneliness disappeared, their feeling of security returned, and they were ready to tell me about their day. They would follow me about, chattering, relaxed, and no longer afraid that they had lost their mother, as they had their father, who had just kissed them good-bye one morning and ridden off, never to be seen by them again.

After supper dishes were done and we had fed the hens in the little enclosure by the barn, had poured milk into the pan for the kitty, we had our baths and were ready for bed. It was story time.

First they said their prayers, the three little girls, and then I read to them—often sitting in the hall so that the children in both bedrooms could hear. When I kissed them good-night they said, "Are you going downstairs now?"

"Yes, but how would it be if I played the piano awhile as you're going to sleep? You can hear me up here, I'm sure."

This satisfied them. I was at home. They knew I'd be there all night. They could sleep peacefully.

CHAPTER TWELVE

Christmas that year was one we have never forgotten. On December twenty-fourth in the early afternoon my neighbor called me to her telephone. We did not have a phone. Wonderingly, I took the receiver.

"Hello, Elsie," came someone's voice over the line. "Mr. Jacobs calling. How about our making it a real Christmas for your children? I'll dress up in a Santa outfit. A bunch of us are coming. We'll get to your house about dark. Oh, say! If you have any presents for the children, put them in the barn. I'll bring them in my pack."

Hardly giving me time to answer, he hung up.

I hurried home and told the children that some people were coming to see us that night. Excitement bubbled in our voices as we changed our clothes and prepared for visitors. The little girls helped me pick out nutmeats for candy. We made a huge plate of divinity and one of chocolate fudge. Company! It was so seldom that we had real company.

About dark our friends began to arrive—Veda and Don Jacobs, the Hansens, the Van Spyks. It was good to see them. In my busy, one-sided world there had been little time for social life.

The children were shy but delighted. Joan was a little cherub with brown ringlets all over her head. Jimmy's crooked grin, so like that of his father, won him attention from all the visitors. With eyes shining, Margie and Marilyn sat in one corner of the davenport and watched. Beverly circulated among the guests. She remembered these people from the days before her father had died. Suddenly she stood transfixed and pointed. "There's Santa out on the front porch looking in the window!"

The big window was low, and we could see Santa plainly as he stood there, his face hidden behind mask and whiskers. He jangled the sleigh bells hanging over his shoulder. Without rapping he burst into the hall and stamped the snow from his feet, making his bells ring joyously. As he came into the room, he unslung his big sack from his back and began to take out gifts. The children's eyes bulged and their mouths dropped open, but they were too dazed to make a sound. Santa talked to them and tried to get them to respond, but they were too amazed to say a word. He distributed the gifts—a red table and chairs for the little girls, presents which had been sent to the children by my brothers and sisters and mother, everything.

Then he stood a moment at the door.

"Ho, ho!" he laughed. "A merry Christmas!" And he was gone with a jingle of sleigh bells.

I looked around at the astonished children. Joan sat in a little red chair and rocked a new dolly with handmade clothes on it. Jimmy pushed a red truck across the floor, making slow progress around so many feet. Marilyn and Margie, still on the davenport, had toys all around them, more than they had seen in their lives before. A hand-knitted stocking cap sat askew on each tousled head. Suddenly Marilyn raised her arms, a purse in each hand, and said slowly, "Well, what's the matter with me? I've got two pocketbooks!"

For years no one could make them believe that there wasn't a Santa Claus.

CHAPTER THIRTEEN

It was a very snowy evening in February that I hurried home from school and found everything so unnaturally quiet. The children did not meet me at the door. Instead, my housekeeper stood there—her face a picture of concern.

"Margie's sick," she said. "She keeps vomiting and cries that her tummy hurts."

On the davenport, Margie turned her white face toward me, and tears of relief—or self-sympathy—rolled down her face. I went to her and pushed the damp hair from her forehead as I kissed her. As I talked to her I put an exploratory hand over her abdomen and pressed gently. When I reached her right side, she winced and cried out sharply. Mentally I diagnosed—no, she's only three—it could not be that. I used my neighbor's telephone to call the doctor in town. When he came and examined her he said curtly, "How soon can you get her to the hospital?"

"Don't you think it could be just a bad stomachache, doctor?"

"We'll run tests in the hospital, but I think my diagnosis is right—an appendix which must come out right away." He was packing his stethoscope into his little black bag as he spoke. "I'll meet you at the hospital," he said brusquely, and was gone.

For a few moments I just stood there beside the davenport, the children looking up at me soberly. Then my thoughts began to click. It was Friday. My housekeeper would be leaving in an hour or so; I must get someone to stay with the children while I went to the hospital with Margie. I would hurry out to my sister-in-law's ranch, a few miles out of Manhattan, and persuade her to come stay with the children. I began to talk to the children as I put on my overshoes, coat, and scarf again.

"I'll be back as soon as I can," I called to my housekeeper as I opened the door. "You'll wait, won't you?"

She nodded, and I hurried out to the car which I kept in one stall of the barn. I had not had it running for several weeks, but the weather had been milder than usual. I filled the radiator with hot water, pulled out the choke, pumped the accelerator a few times, and stepped hard on the starter. With a roar the engine came alive, and I backed the car out into the street. The snow had been scraped from the main highway, and in a few minutes I turned into the driveway that led to Anna's place. I got out to open the gate, but as I tried to drive through the gateway, the car got stuck in the snow. Anna's husband, Joe, saw me and heard the engine as I backed up, taking another run at the deep snow in the driveway, and came to help me. As he shoveled and pushed, we managed to get through the lane to the house. Anna understood my problem as soon as I told her about Margie and was ready in a few minutes to go with me to Manhattan. This time, with a whirl of snow, I whizzed through the gateway and onto the highway, leaving Joe to close the gate after me.

The children were waiting at the door. Still quiet, they followed me about the house as I got Margie ready to go. Finally, with Margie in my arms, I called instructions to Anna, backed out the door, and hurried to the waiting car. Laying her gently in the back seat, I covered her with a blanket, tucked a pillow under her head, and patted her before getting into the front seat under the steering wheel. With a lightness that I did not feel, I talked to her all the while.

The lights of the car, striking the falling snow, lost most of their illumination. Slowly we covered the distance of twenty miles to the hospital. The windshield wiper worked rapidly to push off the thick blobs of snowflakes so that I could see. If only I didn't have to be alone, on a snowy night, with a dangerously sick child! The relief I had at seeing the outlines of the hospital building made me light-headed for a moment.

I carried Margie up the many steps to the front door and down the hall to the elevator. In a ward on the second floor the doctor was waiting. Nurses took blood tests and came back with the results. Yes, the white count was dangerously high, indicating an inflammation in the body.

It was just before midnight when Margie was wheeled into the operating room—such a little form, hardly a bulge under the sheet on the big bed.

"You come in too," the doctor said. "Stay till she is under the anesthetic."

"Oh, I can't," I said quickly, my knees beginning to feel like jelly. I always get so sick with the odor of chloroform or ether. I would disgrace myself and faint dead away just as I had done that other time when I blacked out watching my sister's simple surgery. But Margie whimpered and turned her eyes toward me.

"Of course," I mumbled.

Holding Margie's hand and talking quietly to her, I gripped at consciousness, even though the furniture seemed to go around in waves. At last the doctor motioned to me and nodded toward the door; I made my way from the room. Breathing deeply to clear my lungs of the fumes of ether, I began the lonely vigil in the hall near the operating-room door. The minutes crept by. Before my consciousness paraded all the cases of child appendectomies—the ones that hadn't come out right. I hated the hospital. It was here that Jim had died and Joan had been so sick the year before.

The hall was quiet. If I just had someone to talk with perhaps I could banish my gloomy thoughts. I found a dime in my purse and went to the telephone and called Mrs. Hansen who lived in Bozeman. The sound of her voice made me lose some of my control, and my voice was shaky as I explained about Margie. Then I felt better.

"No, you don't need to come to the hospital. I just needed to hear the voice of a friend to regain my equilibrium. Thank you so much." I hung up the receiver and went back to my post near the operating-room doors.

But in a few minutes the elevator opened and out stepped Mrs. Hansen. My black fears seemed to fade under her friendly assurance. We talked until nurses pushed open the operating-room doors, and we followed Margie's quiet form down the hall to the ward. But I was no longer afraid. I was not alone. Mrs. Hansen stayed with me for a while, and then I begged her to go home. She did. I sat beside Margie's bed and tried not to breathe the ether fumes that came from her lungs.

She stirred at last, sick at her stomach. Her vomiting was hard for me to see. I talked to her. My voice began to penetrate to her consciousness. About four o'clock in the morning she seemed to be sleeping naturally. The nurse put sideboards on her bed. I went downstairs to the lobby and stretched out on a davenport, pulling my coat over me. I slept for about an hour, awakened by the nurse's shaking me.

"Mrs. Doig," she said in a low voice, "your little daughter wakened and tried to climb over the boards on the sides of her bed. Another patient in the room saw her and called to us. We caught her just as she started to fall to the floor. Someone will have to be with her. She's calling for you."

I went with her to Margie's ward and sat by her bed. I whispered to her so as not to awaken the others in the ward. I talked about the mother cat asleep in the barn at home, about old Bo the ranch dog, about the little chickens we had had last summer. She slept again, and I dozed in my chair. Morning came slowly.

After the nurse had given Margie a bath, she brought in breakfast—some milk and a bowl of jello. Margie ate little. All day I sat by her bed, my nearness keeping her quiet. I really could not afford special nurses, and I knew Anna would take good care of the other children. During the night when she slept I dozed. Early the next morning I drove home to see the children and to get clean clothes. That night I returned to be with Margie.

Margie's nurse—the nurse in her ward—told me of the hours I had been gone.

"It's difficult to explain, but she seems to draw herself together and just exist while you are gone. Then she relaxes when you are here. Doctor gave me orders to do several things on her chart when you returned, but not until you were here."

The next morning I went home early, taught the day's school, and returned to the hospital as soon as my pupils had been dismissed. I managed to meet the doctor on his evening rounds.

"Is she doing all right?" I asked, pointing to Margie.

"Oh, yes, fine."

"Is there any chance that I could take her home and bring her back to have her stitches taken out later? I must teach every day," I said.

He said nothing for a few minutes, walked to her chart, which he examined without speaking.

"Yes, Mrs. Doig," he said, "I think I will let you take her home. Be very careful of her for a few days." And he gave me details for her special care.

Getting her clothes from a closet, the nurse gently dressed Margie and soon had her ready for me. I picked her up in my arms and carried her to the elevator, then down the steps of the hospital. Leaving her there in the warm car, I ran back up into the waiting room and the business office where I paid my bill. Folding the papers as I ran I hurried to the car, and we were soon on our way home.

"Mommy," Margie said to me as we started down the road, "Doctor said he was going to put a zipper in me. He didn't, did he?"

"No, dear," I answered as I shook my head and smiled. "He was just teasing."

When we reached home, I again picked her up and gently carried her in to the waiting children. She seemed awfully precious to me, this little burden of mine.

CHAPTER FOURTEEN

The bombing of Pearl Harbor brought rapid changes in our whole country, but I was only a little aware of them at first. Rumors arose that our armies were to be sent to the other part of the world. My brother Wilmer, who was in the army in Fort Lewis, Washington, knew that he would probably be sent overseas soon. His young wife had been teaching at the Dry Creek School since September. Every weekend she spent at our house.

"I think you'd better come out here to be near me until I'm shipped out somewhere," he wrote her during December.

Alma quit her school at Christmas and came to stay with us until he could get a leave to come take her to Fort Lewis. One evening the door opened suddenly, and there stood Wilmer. Alma ran across the room and was almost lost from sight in his big bear hug. She was so petite—not over a hundred pounds—to his bulk.

"You managed to get a leave?" I said.

"Well, not really. The sergeant said that if I didn't get back by Monday it would cost him his stripes."

It was very late before we quit talking and went to bed. The next day Wilmer worked on the old car he had left at my place. He brought the tires and wheels from the barn where he had stored them. With great difficulty he finally started the motor, filled the radiator with alcohol so that it would not freeze, and worked on the engine. The car had no windshield wiper, no heater, no defroster. The weather was bitter cold.

Toward evening we began to heat two big stones. Wilmer fastened two candles to the top of the dashboard. He would light them and keep them burning to keep the windshield from freezing over. The thermometer dropped steadily. I watched it and shook my head.

Wilmer and Alma put on clothes and more clothes. At midnight when they were ready to go I glanced at the thermometer again.

"Forty degrees below zero; that's too cold. Don't you think you should wait until morning?"

Wilmer shook his head. "Promised to be back," he said.

Wrapping the hot stones in burlap sacks, we put them on the floor of the front seat of the car, set a lantern there, piled in several heavy blankets and some food that could be eaten easily. Clumsily they got into the car, their heavy clothing encumbering each movement. For a second my eyes misted over. It might be my last visit with Wilmer. But I had no premonition then that his company, the 163rd Infantry, would be the first to be sent overseas, the first to engage in offensive combat with the Japanese in New Guinea.

Wilmer raced the motor, listened to it, lighted the candles. Alma pulled the blankets closely around her and Wilmer—except for his accelerator foot—and snuggled beside him. The icy snow crackled as they drove away.

I stood and watched the red taillight growing smaller. I looked up into the star-filled sky, looked to the north and saw flashes of northern lights. I shivered from the cold as I walked into the house and shut the door.

After a quick run to the basement to check the furnace I went up to my warm bedroom. As I undressed I thought of McDonald Pass, where they would cross over the Continental Divide. Would the snow plows have shoveled enough space for cars to travel? But I was so weary that I was soon asleep.

A few days later a postal card came with Wilmer's scribbly handwriting on it. "We made it over the pass okay; had to stop a few hours in Drummond. So glad I brought Alma out here with me." It was signed with a pet name we had called him when he was a child—"Pedro."

CHAPTER FIFTEEN

Now and then I still had qualms about my decision to keep all five of the children. One day, when I had left all five in the car for a few minutes while I ran into a store, I came back to find a man and woman peering in at the children.

With a wag of his head the man said facetiously, "Are these all yours, or is there a picnic?"

I knew the old joke, so I quipped right back at him, "They're all mine, and it ain't no picnic." Quickly I drove away, but I was disturbed.

I was keenly aware of the children's lack of a father. I talked of Daddy now and then, not sadly—almost as if he were not too far away. These babies were so lacking in parent-association, I felt.

On Saturdays I made home-baked bread and cinnamon rolls. The little girls pulled chairs up to the table where I kneaded the dough, watched me shape the bread into loaves, spread some of the dough out on the breadboard, spread with butter, sprinkle with sugar and cinnamon, roll up and slice off and put into a pan that had already been given a thick layer of brown sugar.

"Your daddy really liked cinnamon rolls," I told them as I spooned a little thick cream on the top of each roll. "He called them 'cinnamon biscuits.' I suppose that was the Scottish way of saying it. He always asked me to plan to bake them so that they would still be hot when he came in from riding." For our supper we ate the fresh rolls and drank tall glasses of milk.

Sometimes I would question the wisdom of my trying to

rear the children by myself. "They need a father," I would say to myself, feeling a sense of depriving them of their rightful heritage.

That year in the school something happened that restored my confidence in my decision. The fifth grade teacher, Miss Benton, was called Spunky. The nickname fitted her—she was so filled with the love of life and had so many ideas. She moved quickly and spoke succinctly.

"Up the stairs, you," she would say to a pupil. "On the double." And he knew she meant it.

Students in her room respected her, adored her. She was out on the playground every recess and noon, whether it was her turn or not. If it was baseball weather, she was the umpire, standing behind the catcher, her feet far apart, calling out, "Safe on first," or "Ball two." Those boys—girls too—played ball as if their school career depended on it.

If a student could not hit the ball, she would leave her position, run over beside him, pick up the bat and say, "Now, Jack, watch me. See how I put my hands on the bat. Watch me swing it. Now you try." She would stand there and coach him until the ball went sailing out in the field.

Now and then Spunky took a turn at bat. The fielders scrambled backward as fast as they could run.

"I want a good one," she would yell at the pitcher, "straight over the plate," as she gave her bat a few practice swings.

The crack of the bat on the ball and the howls of the fifth graders let us know Miss Benton had hit a "homer."

In the classroom she was queen of her domain. She attacked geography and fractions with the same verve she showed on the playground. Her class ranked high on the scholarship tests at the end of the semester.

One day I saw what occurred when any student questioned her authority. Hearing a sharp rap on my classroom door, I hurried in that direction. Before I could reach the door, Spunky had opened it, stood there—rigid—her eyes shooting out sparks of fire. She jerked her head to the right and waited a second for me to follow her. She walked over to the little bell room where the janitor kept his supplies and where dangled the end of the big rope leading to the bell on top of the building. In the semidarkness I detected a boy from her room, standing there looking fixedly at the opposite wall. Spunky closed the door.

"Law requires that we have a witness for this," she said as she took from a shelf a paddle about two feet long. "All right, young fellow, grab your ankles."

Instantly he assumed the bending position. She swung the paddle with the same agility that she had the bat. There were three sharp cracks.

"That's all," she said to the boy and held open the door for him to leave.

She laid the paddle on the shelf and dusted her hands together as she said, "Well, that's that. Thanks, Mrs. Doig."

The incident was closed. I did not ask the cause of the punishment. Knowing her rapport with her students, I was sure that it was deserved and that the student knew the justice of the action.

Several times after school, Spunky peeked in at my open door. If it was late and my own children had come to "walk Mommy home," she came on into the room. She talked to them, talked to me about them. The little girls were shy, having so little experience with anyone except me and the housekeeper. But she liked to talk to me about my family.

She was a happy, bouncy person. When she said, "Hi,

there," her voice gave me a sort of tingly feeling. It carried that good-to-be-alive convincing tone.

It must have been sometime in March that she stopped by my door after school, walked slowly into the room, and dropped onto a student's desk.

"Mrs. Doig," she said abruptly, "I've had a most dreadful experience. I feel that you will understand. Anyway I must tell someone or I'll burst."

She looked away from me, out the window toward town. "You knew that my dad died last week, didn't you?"

I nodded. "He had been sick a long time, hadn't he? Surely you . . ."

She interrupted me with "Yes, I know, but before he died he told me something I had never known before. He was not my real father. He and Mom adopted me. I never knew that."

I started to speak, but she went on.

"My cousins—I always thought they were my cousins—you know, the ones in Livingstone, they're not my cousins—not even related to me. Why, I've always been as close as sister to them all." Again she paused and continued to stare out the window.

"My own parents are in Butte—oh, yes, they're both still living. They let *me* be adopted because they didn't want me. I have two brothers. They kept the boys but gave me away."

She stopped again. I was silent too. Then she continued.

"After Dad's funeral, I drove here to Manhattan, went to my apartment; I walked the floor all night. Then I got into my car and drove to Butte and searched until I found my own parents. My dad had kept some correspondence with them—he had given me their address. They had seen pictures of me and recognized me. I talked to them. But

I couldn't ask them what was burning my insides out—why did they give me away? Why me?"

For a moment I thought she was going to cry. She cleared her throat and shook her head.

"I can't stand it. It just tears me apart. I don't care what happens to me now."

I put my hand on her shoulder, but she shook it off and stood abruptly. She walked out of the room without even looking back. In a daze I stacked the papers on my desk and put away the books, shaking my head back and forth as she had done, trying to clear my thinking.

It was several days before I saw Spunky again. Curtly she said, "Hi," and ran up the stairs and out of sight. We missed her on the playground. Her students quarreled over the rules of the games or sat about during the recess periods.

After school at night, she refused to be drawn into our teacher gab sessions. The third grade teacher told us Spunky was spending all her free hours at the beer joint. "A fellow there—no good saddle bum—is seen with her all the time. She goes off weekends with him," was the gossip.

Just two weeks before school ended, the janitor poked his head into the doorway of my room one morning before school time.

"Hey! Hear about Spunky?"

I shook my head.

"Run off with that gink she's been hanging around with—quit the school. Got a substitute in to finish the term."

"Did she marry this fellow?"

"Don't know. Suppose so. What in the world ever happened to that gal? She was my favorite of the whole crew of you." With a wave of his hand he was gone toward the bell room.

"This is preposterous!" I said to myself. "Why am I comparing this situation to my own problem? I tried to make myself give away one of my children—almost succeeded. Am I glad I didn't!"

This experience convinced me that it was right to try to keep all my children—together.

CHAPTER SIXTEEEN

The year of 1941-1942 wore on. We were in the war and fighting defensively, steadily, heartbreakingly, losing at each place. We lost Bataan, the Philippines. . . . Fortunately our radio didn't work much of the time. The children were too small to be frightened constantly with the war news.

But the war affected us in various ways. I spent extra time at the school helping register people for sugar stamps, for gasoline rationing. The school board decided we should finish school weeks earlier so the older students could work. We held school on Saturdays. This really cut down on my time with the children, but I spent my evenings with them.

Always, after each one had said her prayer, I sat on the edge of a bed and read stories or retold old tales that they enjoyed. One evening I stopped for a moment in the middle of a story to let the noisy, whistling train go by.

"Mother, why are you stopping?" Beverly asked seriously.

"To wait until that screaming train has passed."

"I can't hear the train," she said.

I turned to the older twins. "You can hear it, can't you?"

They nodded their heads. Not wanting to alarm Beverly I went on with my story, kissed each one good-night, and turned out the light. I went downstairs to correct papers but could not keep my mind on the words I was reading. Of course I knew that Beverly's tonsils were much enlarged. She had had several bouts with tonsilitis. But this hearing business was serious.

The next day I managed to get her into the doctor's office after school for a checkup.

"You're right about the hearing," he said. "The diseased tonsils and adenoids are the cause. They must come out soon or there may be permanent damage."

It all sounded so cool and calm as it fell from the doctor's lips.

"But how can I do it?" I asked. "I must teach Saturdays now. There's no possibility—oh, we do have one Saturday free—the third one in April." I was thinking out loud and taking a busy doctor's time.

"I could call your own doctor in Bozeman and have him schedule the surgery for that date," he offered.

Quickly I accepted and thanked him as I hurried out of the office.

The days moved by slowly because of my anxiety about Beverly. Now I could recognize the symptoms of lack of hearing. Carefully I guarded Beverly against a cold which would bring a flare-up of tonsilitis and prevent the operation. When my free Saturday came, I was up before daybreak, getting her ready, starting the old car, putting blankets and a pillow in the back seat, trying to speak calmly to the twins about what was going to happen to Beverly.

"And when she comes home, can she hear okay again?" Marilyn asked.

"The doctor thinks so," I promised as I told them good-bye, said a few words to my housekeeper who had offered to stay with the children this Saturday, and took Beverly into the front seat of the car with me.

All the way to Bozeman I talked to Beverly about the big hospital and the nurses "like Auntie Irene" and her own Doctor Kittern. I think I convinced her that everything was all right. But it was hard to convince myself when I was shaking a bit inside.

I knew the nurses in the front office of the hospital. I ought to—I had been there so often. Going up in the elevator was fun for Beverly. Then putting on a hospital gown "just like Margie wore in February" absorbed her interest.

When it was time to go into the operating room the doctor motioned to me to come along. Reluctantly I followed. As the nurses wheeled Beverly into the room, he said, "I want you to stay until she's under the anesthetic."

"But you know how sick it makes me. Hadn't I better . . ."

He broke in brusquely. "It will be better for Beverly if you do."

That was that! I talked quietly to Beverly as the strong scent of ether filled my nostrils and my head reeled. It seemed long before the doctor nodded that I could go. Moving rapidly, I left the room and went to the nearest bathroom where I vomited awhile. Never can I have a lady-like reaction such as swooning dramatically at an opportune moment. No . . . I have intense diarrhea or toss up all my cookies.

My upset had quieted somewhat by the time Beverly was wheeled out of surgery and into the recovery room. I stood beside her very still body and waited, but as she puffed out the ether I made repeated visits to the bathroom. By noon she had regained consciousness and lay quiet between vomitings. After a while I said coaxingly, "Do you want some ice cream, dear?"

She shook her head. Ice cream was a seldom-experienced treat at our house. I had promised her any kind she wanted.

The afternoon moved slowly until about five o'clock. Suddenly I realized that the doctor had said I could take her home with me. Then I began to get scared. I asked the doctor many questions.

"You must watch for hemorrhaging," he said. "It may be internal. Her pulse will be slow, her breathing very light. She may even gag on the blood."

He wasn't calming my alarm, but I didn't want him to know what a coward I was. With Beverly in my arms, I went down the elevator and past the front office, where I stopped long enough to pay the bill. At the car I put Beverly in the back seat, her head on the pillow, and covered her with a blanket.

"It hurts so bad, Mother," she whispered.

"I know it does, but it will get well soon. And then you will be able to hear everything again."

As I drove home, I sang songs to her and told her stories.

The center of attention when we arrived home, Beverly was too listless to notice. Margie wanted to tell her about her appendix operation. Each one wanted to see inside her mouth as they had looked at Margie's incision, but Beverly just lay quietly while they buzzed around her.

I carried her upstairs into her room. Laying her on her bed, I stopped a minute to stretch my aching arms.

"Would you like a drink of water, Beverly?"

She shook her head.

"Just wash your mouth with a bit of water and then spit it out."

The children had followed me up the stairs. Margie hurried to the bathroom for the water. Marilyn brought a washpan. Jim and Joan watched silently as Beverly obediently took a little water in her mouth and tried to spit it out. It drooled over her face.

"I can't swallow, Mother," she whispered.

"I know, dear, but it will soon be better. You can close

your eyes and say your prayer to yourself while we kneel down and say ours."

"I'll be first," Marilyn said.

Everyone in bed, I undressed and lay down. Suppose I should fall asleep and Beverly would need me? A very foolish thought that was! Quietly I listened to the even breathing of the children. Restlessly Jim rolled and twisted. He never slept long at one time. Taking my flashlight I got up to cover him, then walked softly into the girls' room. I stooped over Beverly's bed and listened to her breathing. The pungent odor of ether was still there. Having straightened her blankets, I went back to my bed. These acts I repeated often, but I could not sleep. About midnight, I decided to count Beverly's pulse. It seemed so slow. I put my finger on my own wrist. "One, two, three, four. . . ." Why, it was many times faster than Beverly's. I tried to count her respiration. It was so slow and light. Again I felt her pulse. Slower, it seemed! Then my own—I became panicky. The doctor had said to watch out for hemorrhage!

Suddenly I realized it wasn't Beverly's pulse that was slow, it was mine that was fast. I sat on the edge of her bed until I had calmed down. At last I went to sleep for a few hours.

The next day, Sunday, the older twins went to Sunday school alone. Jim still could not walk alone. Joan was too unsure on her feet. The little girls came back chattering about the story they had heard. Beverly still sat quietly in a chair and wouldn't try to eat at all. This kept on all week. I worried during the day as I taught my classes. She would take only liquid, and just a small amount of that.

Saturday evening I knew I must do something. Beverly had lost nine pounds, I discovered, when I persuaded her to stand on the scales, and that was too much for a five-year-old. She was becoming dehydrated. Sitting down on one of the chairs in the kitchen, I motioned for her to come to me and took her on my lap. This was always a signal for the others to gather round. Even Jimmy put down his toys and came to the side of my chair.

"Beverly," I said soberly, "you must eat. I know it hurts, but if you don't eat you'll get weaker and weaker and then I'll have to take you to the hospital. . . ."

Her eyes widened at the last word.

"You've been so brave," I continued. "You haven't cried. Your daddy always said you were his little soldier. Now you must be brave in this way. Every bite you swallow will help you get well faster. Will you try for me?"

She didn't answer, but neither did she shake her head. I turned to the little girls.

"What would she like best? I know—some soft milk toast. We'll put lots of butter on it and warm milk. That will make it slide down easy. Marilyn, you get the bread; Margie, you get the butter. I'll heat some milk."

Putting Beverly down I started up the fire in the old cookstove, added kindling and some larger wood, wiped clean a place on the top of the stove so that I could toast the bread there, poured some milk into a small pan. The children followed me about as we prepared the food. Always they sensed a crisis and became very quiet.

With the fragrant toast in a bowl, I pulled a chair up to the table and again took Beverly on my lap. I began to coax the bites into her mouth. Never had I coaxed my children to eat. Often I had said, "They eat like five little pigs at a trough, each one afraid that if he doesn't eat quickly he'll miss his share."

"That's all I can swallow," Beverly finally said.

89

The bowl was partly empty. I spooned the remaining bites into the waiting mouths of the other children around me.

At frequent intervals all day Sunday, I took time to persuade Beverly to eat some soft food. By Monday there was some color in her cheeks. In a few days her hearing was improving, she was eating normally and running about as usual, a happy little girl.

CHAPTER SEVENTEEN

Somebody—I don't remember who it was—gave me the money and the idea to take a trip to Missouri to see my mother the spring of 1942. The couple who had been living in the station house promised to stay there until I returned. Our preparations for the journey were simple. I washed all the children's clothes and packed them into the old suitcase and a box. One shoe box I filled with fried chicken, another with sandwiches. I put apples and cookies into a brown paper sack.

"I better carry the sack, hadn't I, Mother?" Beverly said. "I'll be extra careful. Margie and Marilyn can each carry a box."

We drove to Anna's ranch and persuaded her to come with us to the railroad station at Logan. This way she could take our car and have it so she could meet us when we returned.

Our train was late. The children ran around while we waited, back and forth on the wooden platforms outside the depot.

"Let them get plenty of exercise before they have to be penned up on a train for thirty-six hours," Anna said. "But they're coughing a little, aren't they?"

"Yes. I took them to the doctor yesterday to have them checked because there are some cases of whooping cough in the neighborhood. The doctor said their coughs didn't sound like that—told me not to worry."

"It's coming! It's coming!" The children raced into the depot and pointed to red lights blinking down the tracks. Each one picked up a package.

With my purse under one arm and the suitcase in that hand, I grabbed the rope that was tied around the big box and herded the younger twins before me as I moved out on the platform to board the train. Margie and Marilyn crowded close to my skirts. Beverly came last.

"I'll be here to meet you in two weeks," Anna called.

The children were so excited that I had to tell them to say good-bye to Auntie Anna. The train was almost full. The brakeman directed us into the club car where we found our double seat—three of us in each seat. There were no children in this car—mostly men. The train started with a jerk which started the girls giggling. As it began to move more smoothly, the children crowded at the window to look out.

"There goes Manhattan," Beverly called. We had had to go to Logan to catch the through train.

The first hours went by rapidly because of the interest and excitement. Everything was so new, so different. We ate our lunch, and the children leaned back against the seats and relaxed. In a few minutes they were asleep, propped against each other, Beverly and the older twins in one seat; Jim and Joan and I in the other. I stretched Jim out on the seat, his head one way, Joan with her head the other, and got up to walk around.

When they awoke I was ready for them with some cut-out-and-paste-in pictures. By evening I noticed that they were all coughing more frequently, but there was no whooping. I had asked the doctor about whooping cough shots, but he had advised against them. "Still in the experimental stage," he had said.

As soon as it was dark, I took a blanket out of the box and spread it on the floor between the seats. Here I put three of them and covered them with their coats. The other two lay on the seats. I hovered around them most of the time, going back and forth between them and the ladies' room, concerned about their coughing. By morning their coughs were longer and more drawn out. I felt sick inside— worried about the children, embarrassed before the other passengers. I knew it was the beginning of whooping cough. As soon as a child would start to cough I would hurry her to the rest room, trying to keep her away from people. I could not force myself to look at the other travelers.

By afternoon the children could not keep any food in their stomachs. I avoided the stares of the people as I made my way back and forth from our seat to the ladies' room. About four o'clock I looked at my watch and said, "Almost there now. Will you children sit quietly while I go brush my hair and put on some lipstick?"

They nodded, their eyes solemn. I hurried down the aisle thinking, "Well, there's nothing left in their stomachs. Surely they'll be okay." I felt relieved. We would be there in a very short time.

A few minutes later I came back. While I had been gone a kind old gentleman had given each of the children a ripe banana. Of course they had eaten because they were hungry. But immediately their coughing had caused them to up-chuck everything. The remainder of the trip I scrubbed the floor.

When the train finally reached our destination, we wearily picked up all our things and hurried off the car, not even taking one embarrassed glance backward at the people we were leaving.

My sister met the train, gathered the children into the car, and said as we drove away, "What's the matter, Elsie? You look disturbed, and the children are so pale."

"Whooping cough!" I groaned. The words were a signal for every child to start coughing. "I think I scrubbed every inch of the aisle in our car of the train. Oh, why did I ever try to come?"

"It'll be all right," she said, and then added, "Someday you'll even laugh when you remember this."

She laughed as I told her details of the trip. Years passed before I could find anything humorous about it.

CHAPTER EIGHTEEN

Immediately after my return from Missouri, the children and I packed necessary belongings and furniture and moved out to the little log house at Dry Creek for the summer. Easily we settled into the familiar home. The children looked for accustomed haunts—the dirt pile behind the oil shed, the straw nests in the log garage, a few old toys here and there. The girls set up doll-housekeeping on the screened-in porch.

Early in May we had made a trip out here to plant the garden. Alden let me use the potato patch space down by the south pasture entrance. It was easy to irrigate. The soil was rich and crumbly. The little girls dropped chunks of seed potatoes in the first rows that I hoed open. Radishes and lettuce and other small seed I had to plant, but the children carefully closed the open rows, using their hands and feet. One by one we planted the early vegetables.

By the time we arrived in late May the weather was warm enough for us to put in later vegetables. With Jimmy and Joan in the little wagon, the sack of seeds wedged beside them, the girls and I went down the road west for a quarter of a mile. A turn to the left, on down the road south, and we were at the gate, a very tough one to open and shut. With one arm around the post and the other around the gate, I tugged and pulled at the tight wire that was looped over to keep it shut. I gave up and took the children out of the wagon. We all crawled under the wires, shoved the wagon under, and reassembled on the other side of the fence. Soon we were at the garden spot.

The quiet of the place was restful—no sounds but those

of nature. A red-winged blackbird called to his mate from his swaying perch on the willows along the banks of the stream close by. The water gurgled softly as it moved over the rocks and brushed against the banks. After we had finished our planting, we took off shoes and stockings and waded in the little creek. It was good to look back at the rows of patted earth of the garden-to-be and think of food for the family.

Again I milked one of my two cows that Alden still cared for during the winter. We had milk and butter, cream and cheese a-plenty.

Planning ahead on supplementing our meat stock, I bought chickens—little day-old cockerels, the cheapest to get. For a few weeks we kept them in pasteboard boxes in the kitchen, making them warm at night by putting half-gallon jars of hot water in with them. Always I set my alarm for midnight and looked to see that the reservoir of the stove was filled with hot water before I went to bed. When the ringing of the alarm dragged me out of bed, I stumbled into the kitchen, emptied and refilled the jars, pushed the huddled chickens apart so that I could set down the warm jars, covered the boxes almost over, and went back to bed.

As the chickens grew, the girls helped me put them in a little enclosure near the garage where we had cut a hole through the logs, giving them a place to sleep at night. The children made many trips each day from the house to the chicken pen, sometimes to carry scraps from the kitchen or water for the pans—often just to watch the active little chicks.

The service station trade had diminished during our absence, but our income from it paid for the groceries and for Madeline to stay with us that summer. She had been student teacher for me during the school year in Manhattan. The children adored her.

Every Sunday evening the neighbors gathered in the pasture across the way for a ball game. I stocked the cellar with cases of pop, the show cases with gum and candy and crackerjacks. Saturday evening I filled the refrigerator with bottles of pop and two tubs with cold water where I submerged as many bottles as I could get under the water. Sometimes we sold thirteen cases of pop to the thirsty crowd. On Mondays my arms ached and my back was sore, but there was money in the till to restock the station and enough left over to pay our bills.

In July I heard of a vacancy in a high school seventy miles away; a music and English teacher was needed. Just what I wanted! I applied and was accepted. We made the trip up into the mountains, over the pass, and down into the town. I was able to rent a house for the school year. Everything now began to be geared to September first.

During the warm summer days I sewed, making school dresses for Beverly, who would be six in October, shirts and trousers for Jimmy, play clothes for the twins, and pajamas for everyone.

As the garden began to produce, I started the unending work of canning—forty quarts of peas, the same of beans and of corn. I bought baskets of peaches and pears and plums. The boxes of jars piled up in the cellar, and still I canned.

By the last week of August I began final preparations for our leaving. Tomatoes had grown prolifically; they hung big and green on the vines but only a few had ripened. We picked baskets of them, wrapped each one in the papers which had been around the peaches, and packed them in boxes. One day we took the car to the gate near the garden and spent the whole day there. We pulled the carrots and packed them in clean, dry sand we had brought from the river nearby. Each little girl had her task. Beverly pulled the carrots, Margie carried them to the baskets and laid them in the layer of sand. Marilyn, with her little shovel, made sure there was sand between each layer of carrots. We pulled the yellow Spanish onions and laid the golden globes in the sun to dry, tugged away at the cabbage roots until they came out of the ground, and tied a string to the root of each one. With the spade I dug up the hills of potatoes; Margie and Marilyn and Beverly all worked to carry the "spuds" as they called them to the gunny sacks which Joanie was supposed to hold open for them. All of this we loaded into the car and brought to the cellar at the station.

The last day before we were to leave for the school, I dressed the chickens—now almost full-grown roosters. Madeline took the children down to the Dry Creek school yard that afternoon to play on the slides and teeter-totter. Killing all their chickens would seem needlessly cruel to them, I was sure—it did even to me. A neighbor stopped for gas, and I persuaded him to chop off the heads of the young roosters. Hour after hour I plucked feathers from the dripping fowls which I had immersed in boiling water. As I cut open and dressed the chickens, the penetrating odor nauseated me. I could not eat supper. By evening I had the cooled and wrapped meat packed tightly in the refrigerator which I set at the lowest possible temperature.

Very early in the morning we were ready to be off. A truck was backed up to the kitchen door, and we tugged and lifted until everything was stowed in or tied on. The truck left first, and we followed closely so we could watch the load carefully.

As we started down the road, I turned to look back at the little log house. The gas pumps were locked and empty, the doors and windows curtainless. That familiar little sense of loneliness—or was it uncertainty of the future—tugged at my consciousness for a moment. Then I turned back to the road ahead wondering what the coming school year held for us.

CHAPTER NINETEEN

"Here comes that pretty little widow!" called the janitor as I unlocked the door of my classroom one morning.

A widow! Of course I was, but somehow I resented the term every time it was attached to me. The "pretty" was exaggerating, I suppose, but the "little" fit. The week Jim died I had lost twelve pounds. I continued to streamline my figure with my endless activity until I wore a size thirteen, then a twelve. Clothes had been a real temptation for me when I was an unmarried teacher, but on my present slim budget—paying a housekeeper half my wages, six of us living on the other half, and no wages at all during the summer—new clothes were an impossibility.

Fortunately two of my sisters were the same size as I. Maylo was on the faculty of the University of Syracuse; Irene lived in Boston, the wife of a successful physicist. They sent me dresses that they had tired of. With very little altering, the clothes fit. One dress I remember well— a beautifully tailored green corduroy with a tiny leather belt. Another was a black wool gabardine, complete with lapel pin. Shoes, hats, coats—oh, I was lucky. Clothes I could not use for myself I made over for the children. I could hold my head high, proud that I looked as well-dressed as the other teachers. But widow! That "stuck in my craw."

In this little mountain town we were strangers. When I had come to find a place to live for the school year, I had found only one house available for us to rent—a small gray house. It squatted flat on the ground with the doorsills level with the turf. Lack of plumbing necessitated the use of an outdoor toilet and galvanized washtub for our baths. The two bedrooms were very small.

We drove the big truck into the yard and began to unload the furniture and box after box of jars of canned vegetables and fruit. We jammed what furniture we could into the four little rooms and left the remainder of it on the truck to return to the valley. The boxes we piled on the ground beside the kitchen, trying to figure where we could stow them away.

Joe, my brother-in-law, had driven the truck. He found a trapdoor in the middle of the kitchen floor. Lifting the ring fastened to the wood, he raised the heavy door. Below we found a hole—a cellar of sorts—about six feet deep. A ladder led into it. One at a time, we investigated the possibility of putting shelves in it and storing our vegetables and canned stuff there. Seemed impossible, but I was used to attempting the impossible. A trip to the hardware store-lumberyard and we had enough boards to make space for the jars of string beans, peas, corn, and fruit. Our backs ached as we carried down the last baskets of carrots and potatoes and hung cabbages from nails we had pounded on the two-by-fours, but we beamed with satisfaction as—hours later—we squeezed around the little kitchen table to eat supper.

But the house was very inadequate. A pump in the kitchen was fastened to a linoleum covered table beside a small tin sink, under which was a bucket that had to be emptied frequently. An old wood-and-coal cookstove and a pot-bellied heater in the living room would warm only a small part of the house during the severe winter.

Standing in the front doorway, I looked down the street about two blocks to a pretty little stucco house with green shutters. I knew it was empty. I had been told that I could not rent it because I had children, but foolishly I had called Mr. Quentin, the owner, to be sure. His wife answered. "Only married with no children," she had said emphatically.

Turning back into the little gray house, I sighed as I opened the davenport for a bed for Beverly.

But we were happy. The autumn sun warmed our little yard. I bought a rope and made a swing on two of the clothesline poles. We were near the schoolhouse, and I did not have to drive the car. Often we would walk to the edge of town where we would skip stones in the crystal-clear water of the Madison River. The water was swift and cold, but we took off our shoes and stockings and waded near the bank or tossed little rocks into the foaming water.

My schedule at school was a heavy one—the high school band and glee club, all of the grade music, and four classes of high school English. I studied late at night to read the textbooks and prepare for my lessons. There was no time to worry about inconsequential trifles!

It was late in November that I received the message from Mr. Quentin. The principal at the high school passed it on to me.

"Oh, Mrs. Doig," he called to me as I passed his open office door, "Mr. Quentin called. Wants you to stop by his house when you have time. You know where he lives?" He looked up at me quizzically as he swiveled his chair around. Did he have an unusual quirk to his smile?

"Yes," I said, "it's that big brick house on Main Street, isn't it?" I waited for his nod and hurried on to my waiting class.

It was after I had gone home from school that I thought of the message again.

"Oh, Anna Mae," I called to my housekeeper, "keep your fingers crossed. Mr. Quentin sent a message to me to come see him. Maybe we'll get that house yet—you know, the empty one down the street. I'm going to see him right now. Don't wait supper for me."

As I hurried across town I kept saying to myself, "Now don't get your hopes up; don't get your hopes up."

The doorbell's ringing brought Mr. Quentin to answer my call. He was a man of sixty or more, well-dressed, smooth pink cheeks, a bald head away back to a rim of hair above his collar line. He was effusive in his welcome. I've misjudged these people, I thought. But his wife had seemed so cross, so unfriendly. "Will you come in?" he said. He moved back into the hall and opened another door and stood aside for me to enter. Awkwardly clutching my purse, I moved into the room, then stood transfixed, staring at a magnificent brown stag which looked at me from its large, lifelike eyes from velvet tapestry which reached from the baseboard almost to the ceiling.

"You like my tapestry?" His voice warmed with pleasure. He moved into the room. "Won't you sit there?" and he indicated a velvet upholstered chair of deep gold color and then sat down himself.

I looked around the room. I was unacquainted with such luxury.

"My own room," Mr. Quentin said. "Would you like a drink?"

Before I could shake my head, he had pressed a button or moved something and a piece of furniture which looked like a desk opened into a bar. Rows of bottles and glasses appeared.

"What would you like?" He picked up a bottle.

"Oh, no, thank you, I don't drink." But I gazed fascinatedly at the little private bar.

"If you don't mind, I'll have something." He was already pouring some amber-colored liquid into a glass.

My eyes went back to the tapestry as I waited for him to finish his drink. "How real it looks!" I said. "I have a velvet tapestry, but not nearly the size of that one."

He set down his glass and rubbed his hands together and put them to his chin.

"Now, let's see. Mrs. Doig, you wanted to rent our little stucco house on your street, didn't you? Would you still be interested?"

"Oh, yes," I said eagerly, "but your wife said, 'No children,' and I still have my five." I smiled ruefully.

"Well, now, perhaps we might make an exception in your case. Would you like to look at the house?"

From a drawer close by, he took a ring with two keys on it and led the way to his front door and down the walk. His large white hand lingered on my shoulder as he helped me into the car.

The house was a jewel, compact and clean and modern. A living room with a wool rug and a big window, one large bedroom, one smaller one, a gleaming white bathroom, a kitchen with room for a table where we could eat comfortably, and an electric stove.

His hand under my elbow, Mr. Quentin led me to the stairs and down to the basement. A big furnace smiled at me. Central heating! Oh, boy! Rows of shelves in one corner for my canned fruits and vegetables!

"Will the house be big enough? Does it suit you?"

"Oh, if we could only have it! I'll promise to keep the children from marking the walls, from ruining the rug."

"Now—say twenty-five a month for rent," he said. "When could you move in?"

I almost hugged him.

As soon as I had paid the first month's rent in advance I left him. Hurrying home, I think I cried a few tears in sheer happiness. I could hardly wait until I had opened the door to start telling of our good luck. The children caught my excitement and their eyes glowed as I told them all about the house.

We moved in that weekend. Anna and her husband drove up from the valley in their pickup. We made trip after trip from the little low gray house to the new white one. How cozy we were in our new home! The first snow came the following week, but we didn't worry. We were warm and snug, and we didn't even have to go outside to a bathroom.

It was several weeks before I began to have misgivings. Shopping in the only grocery store, I met the Foremans.

"You moved into Mr. Quentin's house, I hear. How'd that happen?" Mrs. Foreman reached for a package of cereal on the top shelf.

"Why, don't you know?" her husband explained. "Mrs. Quentin is visiting their daughter in California for the winter, and you know Mr. Quentin's reputation with the women, especially trim little widows and unattached females."

My face flamed. It wasn't what he said—it was the tone of his voice. There was more than teasing in it. Mr. Foreman smiled, but there was a note of warning as he said, "Keep your doors locked at night, especially the back one."

They moved on toward the front of the store. I stood a second, a box of cornflakes in my hand, looking after them. I shook my head as if to clear it and shrugged my shoulders. Nonsense! But again came the nagging thought. Did he give any real reason for letting us have the house, for changing his mind? The rent was very low, but I thought he was being kind, sympathetic. Must I always be so gullible?

Awakened to these thoughts, I began to remember little snatches of stories about Mr. Quentin, savory bits of gossip—a girl in trouble. His name linked with the incident, a suit over the affair, a fatherless baby. These stories hadn't touched me, did not belong in my world, I thought. But here and now they did mean something. Suspicion once aroused, I was aware of everything I had heard about this man. Mrs. Foreman—the one person I had known before I came to this town—came to see me and told me other tales of this man's reputation. I could no longer ignore them.

I did lock my doors, something I had never done before except when leaving for overnight or longer. Each evening I slid the bolt on the back door carefully, and my mind was troubled. I seemed to read little innuendos of meaning into people's conversations. Some of this I told Anna Mae, trying to laugh at myself and my concerns.

Fortunately this worry was of short duration. About two weeks after we had moved in, as I stood in the post office lobby waiting for the mail to be sorted, I heard the rundown of the local news. One exciting bit stirred my pulses quickly—Mr. Quentin had been taken to a hospital in the valley. His arm was broken. This had happened as he had been getting out of the bathtub. When the doctors examined it and X rayed it, they found that he had cancer of the bone. His wife was summoned. She took him to Rochester.

From the post-office gossip I followed his progress for weeks. His wife was not satisfied with the diagnosis of the hospital at the Mayo Clinic. She tried another on the west coast, took him to specialists everywhere. He was gone all winter. He came back to the little town in the spring—to die.

This may have been the first time that cancer turned out to be the friend of a little widow.

CHAPTER TWENTY

I had noticed her the first day I entered the school in September. She walked quickly past my door—not hurriedly, just determinedly—as if she anticipated her day and enjoyed the anticipation. This glimpse of her gave me the impression of an old dark-blue dress that hung unevenly on a dumpy figure, gray hair in a short, mannish cut, and steel-rimmed glasses which reflected the light coming from my classroom windows as she passed my door. Cleaning woman, I checked mentally, as I looked down at my stylish brown dress and matching shoes.

But I was wrong. When we filed into the home economics room for the teachers' meeting, there she was. I sat looking at her until the principal began to speak.

"If each of you will stand and tell his name and department, we'll be getting acquainted. Miss Werner, you've been here the longest. You start it."

She stood quickly with that all-in-one movement, smiled, spoke distinctly, "Ruth Werner, math," bobbed her head so that the light played on her glasses, and sat down.

My surprise must have been written on my face, for the teacher beside me nudged my ribs gently and whispered, "A queer one, but you'll like her." The teacher speaking stroked her fashionable red suit. "She's an institution in this school. Been here for years and years. She wears well."

For weeks after that I was busy finding my way around the school building, learning to know my students, my classes, the other teachers. I was afraid of making mistakes, because this was my first year of teaching in high school. I wanted to learn, wanted to fit into this school.

I had to make good. My future—my children's future—depended on it.

The surrounding country was beautiful, with towering mountains already snow-capped, cold swift streams, lakes of crystal clear water. The little town was isolated from the Gallatin Valley from which I had come except for the one highway that twisted like a ribbon up the tortuous turns of the mountain pass south of us and over and down the other side. There was not even a railroad into the town. It was a trading place for the ranchers who lived round about.

The days went by easily, linked to each other in a chain of learning. I had much more to learn than the students. For long hours every night, after my children were asleep, I studied texts. During the day I studied the ways of high school students, the customs and procedures of the school. I tried to learn about the teachers, to learn from them also. It was October before I found out much about Miss Werner.

Indian summer came with its golden days. No one accustomed to fall in high altitude was deceived by the warmth and the sunshine, which gave no hint of the not-too-distant approach of early winter. Snow might fall any night, loading the branches with its weight, hiding the bright color of the aspen trees. But each day was savored and enjoyed completely. The sky was blue-blue, with here and there patches of thin clouds like lacy petticoats. Such days would tempt any red-blooded boy of the community to go hunting.

The first day of grouse season came. Two boys were absent from my first-hour English class. Three more were out of my third-hour class. One boy in particular could not afford to play hookey if he expected to get a passing grade. In reporting these absences to Mr. Smith, the guidance director, I said, "These boys should be warned. Their grades can't stand much of this."

"First day of grouse season," he said as he wrote the names on his scratch pad. "Yours isn't the only class they have skipped. Think I'll talk to Miss Werner. She'll know how to cope with them."

The following morning Mr. Smith stopped by my door long enough to call in, "Don't lower those boys' grades for yesterday's truancy. We have a better plan," and then his long legs took him rapidly on down the hall to his office.

Curious about this, I waylaid Miss Werner in the hall at noon. As she spoke to me her smile lighted up her blue eyes behind the steel-rimmed spectacles. I put my hand out to stop her when she started to hurry on after a quick greeting.

"Oh, Miss Werner, did you talk to those boys?"

"Who? Oh, yes." She spoke quickly, almost sharply. "They'll not do it again." Her smile took away any sting of rebuff. Without any more explanation she moved rapidly on to her room.

Standing watching her, I wondered about it all. What influence could that small, unimpressive-looking teacher have on those boys? Inwardly I criticized her rusty-black suit which sagged on both sides, the worn collar of the white blouse that drooped from lack of starch. What could that little old maid know of boys? What kind of teacher could she be? What did it take to make a good teacher?

But the boys did not skip school again in spite of the weather-perfect mornings of the wild duck season which followed soon after grouse season.

One afternoon the "honk-honk" of wild geese drew our eyes to the classroom window. A half-spoken sentence died on my lips as I watched with fascination a large triangle of dark bodies flying along toward the mountain lake about two miles away to the south. The schoolhouse stood on a hill near the edge of town. From the windows we caught a flash of sunlight on the water of the lake. The echelon of geese banked and turned and were soon lost to our view in the brush near the lake shore.

"Will they stay there all night?" I caught myself breaking into the thoughts of the class.

"Yup," a tall senior answered instantly, "and they're big 'uns too. Canadian geese. Up at daybreak with a good shotgun a fellow could soon git his limit."

"How many are you allowed?" I knew I should get back to English, but it was near the end of the last period.

"Two," several voices said at once.

"Can you start shooting at any time?"

The bell rang to end the discussion, but one boy waited a moment to answer my question. Scraps of conversation drifted back to me as the class pushed its way down the hall.

"You going, Tom?"

"Course, but we gotta make it back 'fore nine. I promised Miss Werner. Trig's not easy for me, and I need it if I'm gonna take engineering in college."

"Let's go talk to her."

"I'm goin' anyway, no matter what she says," one voice said belligerently.

The idea of that midget teacher affecting these big six-footers seemed ridiculous. Many of them were rough-looking fellows who lived on the ranches nearby. How could a teacher's control continue on—outside the school hours? Or could it? What did it take?

As the boys straggled into my first-hour class the next day, wild geese were at once the principal topic before the bell rang.

"Git one, Bill?"

"Naw, guess the sun was right in my eyes. How 'bout you?"

"Yeah, first shot. And is he a beauty! Mom's gonna dress him and put him in the freezer. Taste good for Christmas. Hey, Red, any luck?"

"Got two, but, boy, did I get wet! Stepped in a hole and went in over my boots." He slapped his damp Levi's. "Mom said to change clothes, but I told her I'd promised Miss Werner I'd make it here by nine. 'Bout dried out now."

If I could only get that kind of interest in English from them! Searching frantically through the literature book, I looked for a story or poem on hunting or on wildlife. My attention was drawn to "To a Waterfowl," and with a little introduction I began to read:

> Whither midst falling dew
> While glow the heavens with the last steps of day,
> Far through their rosy depths
> Dost thou pursue thy solitary way?

I explained the unfamiliar expressions. "Durned old poetry" as the boys called it was not so hard for them if I made it come alive in a real-life situation. By the time I had reached the last stanza the students were in a somewhat pensive mood and did not even feel affronted by the "teachy-preachy" ending:

> He who from zone to zone
> Guides through the boundless sky thy certain flight
> In the long way that I must tread alone
> Will lead my steps aright.

The morning after the first snow fell I met Miss Werner in the hall.

"Beautiful snow!" she said in way of greeting. Her smile was infectious. "Marvelous deer-hunting weather. Good tracking! Watch those boys. I'll try to get around to seeing all of them sometime today. If Bill Goodin doesn't show up, let me know." And she was on her way toward her room at the end of the hall.

Thank goodness it was Friday!

Saturday afternoon the children and I walked down to the ranger station office near the bridge over the river east of town to watch the cars as they stopped at the station to be checked. Slung across the radiator hood of a car would be a perfect two-year-old buck, or tied to the bumpers might be a five-point deer. Often there were two—one tied over the top of the car. Sometimes I recognized high school boys who poked their heads out of the car windows and called out about their luck. I moved closer to the station to see the person to whom they were speaking. Miss Werner—I might have known!

Monday morning I saw a group of fellows down at the end of the hall, all talking at once, clustered around the little math teacher. As I stood watching, I tried to understand her power over these boys, their rapport with her. Her face was transfigured with her joy and interest. To each boy she seemed to ask the right question. She spoke their language. Each fellow vied with the others in telling of his experiences. Perhaps this was the reason for her success.

In the weeks that followed, the snow became deeper and deeper. Last period of the school day became increasingly difficult to teach. The large classroom across the hall became a popular place. Fifty or more students packed the room and spilled over into the corridor. My class drooled enviously as they watched skis being rubbed with wax, boots pulled on. I found out that anyone with study hall that period could sign up for this ski class. Our science teacher had been a national junior ski champion. Teaching this class was real joy for him.

Not until the students, skis over their shoulders, had clomped noisily down the hall and had been loaded into their station wagons and had taken off for the hills could I draw the attention of my class to the prosaic subject of English.

On Saturdays everyone who could be free drove to ski-jump hill. Children skied on the gentle slopes. The adults came expertly down the steep hills, following the flags of the slalom, or swiftly along the track to the jump, soared into the air, and dexterously landed hundreds of feet away. Those of us who could not ski watched and enjoyed the sport vicariously. The whole community turned out.

The week before Christmas holidays were to begin, a local ski meet was held. Businessmen of the town offered prizes. No one missed this. Even teachers who did not attend any other local gatherings turned up that morning, dressed in their heaviest jackets and snow pants, armed with warm blankets and thermos bottles of hot coffee. My children and I rode with a neighbor. The ten miles up the canyon road had been cleared by the big rotary plow which chewed up the snow and piled it high along the roadside. The bright sun dazzled my vision but gave no warmth as its rays reflected from the deep layer of snow. People hurried out of their cars and crowded as near the ski lift as possible, their breath making little cloudlike puffs as they called greetings to each other. Some of the men tended an open fire. The pungent aroma of burning fir branches filled the air. Youngsters crowded around, holding mittened hands toward the flames.

Shouts of laughter heralded an ignominious flop of a skier into the snow. A sudden hush meant that a skier was in the air off the big jump, then shouts and exclamations as he landed upright and braked himself to stop his race. It was during one of my frequent trips to the fire to warm my fingers and check up on my children that I heard a groan from the group of watchers. Turning I looked toward the ski jump. At its base a crumpled figure made a dark blotch on the snow of the mountainside. Several skiers moved quickly toward the figure. There was a babel of voices, some hushed, some imperatively loud with commands.

"Bring the stretcher!"

"Who is it?"

"What happened?"

"It's Bill, Bill Hanley."

"Bring the toboggan. On the double!"

Carefully the boy was brought down the hill, but as he was lifted onto the stretcher I saw that one leg dangled crazily. It was only a matter of minutes before he was eased into the back of a station wagon. The driver was in the seat, the motor running, and yet the car waited. Someone was calling toward the crowd, "Miss Werner! Oh, Miss Werner!"

The shabby teacher separated herself from the crowd and moved quickly across the snow to the car. In a moment she was inside and the station wagon went slowly down the narrow canyon road.

"Why did she go with them?" I inquired of a fellow standing by.

"Bill asked for her," he explained curtly as if any other answer was unnecessary.

All the way back to town I thought of the incident and what it would mean to be chosen as Miss Werner had been. In his agony of pain and anxiety, Bill had turned to her. Why? That evening I went to get my mail. The post office was filled with people, pushing and jostling each other to get to their boxes. There was much talking about the day's activities. I listened. Bill had been taken to the hospital in the valley below. His leg was broken—a spiral fracture, bone shattered, someone said. An operation had taken a long time. Miss Werner and the boy's father were still with Bill.

"What about his mother?" I asked someone standing near.

"She's been dead since Bill was a small boy. Didn't you know? Bill's father has taken care of the boy alone."

At school on Monday morning I stood in the hall watching the students come and go. I heard the usual buzz of excited voices, scraps of conversation, about the ski meet, about Bill. Miss Werner's faded coat appeared around the corner at the regular time. Briskly she walked down the hall, her head bobbing now and then as she greeted students. No change in her attitude. She fumbled for keys in her old leather purse, unlocked her door, and went into her room. Determined to know more about this woman, I went down the hall, weaving my way in and out of the groups of students. I tapped on her door. With her call of "Come" I entered. At her desk she continued to sort some papers as she looked up inquiringly at me.

"Miss Werner," I said with no preface, "please tell me how you do it."

"Do what?" she said simply. Her friendly smile encouraged me to go on.

"Tell me the secret of your success with the students. Why do they obey you? What control have you over these students, especially the boys?"

"Oh, it's easy, really. I just love them—all of them, from

the biggest, roughest cowboy to the littlest, most unkept urchin—and I let them feel it."

"But how, why?"

"Please sit down, Mrs. Doig, and I'll try to explain as well as I can. I've always loved children, particularly boys. When I was a girl, I planned to have a family of boys of my own after I had married. But I never married, you know. I was engaged to a young fellow when I was a senior in teachers college. We kept putting off the date for our marriage. First my mother died, after a long, very expensive illness. I taught school to help pay the hospital and doctor bills. Then my father's stroke left him partially helpless, and he lived with me for twenty years before he died. Of course I could not marry and leave him. But I found that I did not need to be married to have a family of boys. I have had hundreds of them in my classrooms every school day. I was not long in discovering that high school students need loving. I am partial to boys who have had broken homes, those who have been neglected. In many ways I could make up for some of the lack of love, even of discipline. And I have really tried. Oh, it's not been difficult. I've enjoyed my big family of boys. What a beautiful, full life I have had." She stopped and smiled ruefully. "There's not much of a secret, I'm afraid. If I have had any success it has been due to my interest in these students, real interest—not just a superficial one—I do care what they do, what happens to them. But I think you can spell it all out with one word—love."

She picked up a book from her desk and began to leaf through it.

"Thank you, Miss Werner," I said. Humbled I went back to my work of teaching, a work glorified now somehow by a little math teacher.

CHAPTER TWENTY-ONE

Still in the band-leader uniform, I hurried from the stage and through the crowd to find my children. People stopped me on all sides to tell me how beautiful the operetta had been and how much they enjoyed the band's playing. Fretting with the delay, I managed to nod, smile, and say, "Thank you," but always I edged closer to the seats where I had placed my five children at the beginning of the program.

When I reached them, four pairs of round eyes looked up at me expectantly.

"Where's Jimmy?" I asked, automatically taking count of them. Joan, his two-year-old twin, looked at me sleepily.

"We don't know. He must've gone when we weren't looking," Beverly explained. "He was here; then I looked around and he was gone. And you told us not to go away from this place."

"Mother, we liked the dancers in the black boots," the four-year-old twins chattered almost simultaneously.

"That was the Russian dance," I answered, but my eyes were scanning the milling crowd to see where my son might be.

The gymnasium was still filled with the audience. Doors were opening and closing. I must find him before he slipped out unnoticed. Calling to another teacher to stay with my children, I wove in and out of the heavy coats being put on, brushed against leather jackets, cowboy hats, heard the scraping of high-heeled boots, felt the gusts of frosty air as the doors opened and closed.

Near the doors I saw a group standing, looking at some

object on the floor. With a sigh of relief I wormed my way into the circle. There on the floor sat my son, placidly eating his Christmas candy.

"Jimmy, Jimmy," I scolded, "why did you get yourself lost?"

"Your son's not lost," said a man whom I recognized as the father of my best French-horn player. "It's you who are lost."

The laugh that followed was comradely. It warmed my heart. Besides, here was my son. Picking him up, I talked to the people around me, holding his sticky hands away from the band uniform. I moved slowly to the place where the four other children were waiting.

Snowsuits were soon on and zipped, overshoes on—Beverly could do her own, thank goodness! The teacher who was helping me offered to stay a moment while I brought my car around to the door of the gym. Friendly school parents helped me get the children to the car. With a few words to the janitor about costumes to be put away, I was through for the evening—for the whole two weeks of the Christmas vacation—to go home with my sleepy family.

The children were drowsy when I helped or carried them into the house. My mind was busy with the thoughts of the successful evening as I tucked them into bed. The operetta had been delightful, the performance almost perfect. No one but the teachers knew that two other teachers and I had written all the script ourselves, combining songs and folk dances with our original narrative. We had depicted a shipboard scene with homesick servicemen thinking of their homes and the native customs at Christmastime. The shop teacher had helped, using his classes to make the stage scene of the superstructure of a ship. During gym classes the physical education teacher had taught the grade school students the dances for the operetta. Over two hundred students in the program and not a hitch!

With the children in bed, I sat down for a moment in the quiet living room. This problem that I had pushed to the back of my mind must be attacked. Two weeks had passed since my housekeeper had showed me a letter in which she had been offered a job in the little post office in her home-town.

"I've been given just a week," she said, "before I go to work there. For three years I have been hoping to get this position. There's a vacancy now. If I don't take this I may never get another chance. I really am sorry to leave you in this predicament, but you see how it is."

Yes, I understood. There was nothing I could do except to accept the situation. Now I must find someone to help me. I had scoured the community where I was. No one was available who wanted to do housework and care for five children! In desperation I sent word to Anna, my sister-in-law. She came up on the next bread truck and stayed with me until this afternoon, when she had gone home for Christmas, again riding on the bread truck. We had talked for hours about our coming to the valley to spend part of the holiday with her, of our having time then to find someone who would be my housekeeper. Her confidence gave me assurance and I had shoved this problem aside—to be solved later. Now I must attack it.

As I started to go to bed, I stood a moment looking around me at the room. Everything was so clean. The quiet of the night was so peaceful. A whole two weeks before me now, I thought. How I needed it! In the morning we would plan our vacation days. Right after Christmas Day we would drive down to the valley, visit friends and relatives, go to our own little church in Bozeman. I turned to my bed and was asleep before I could think more.

With morning came the resuming of household duties. The children helped me with the work. About two o'clock in the afternoon two high school boys knocked at the door.

"Hey, teacher, do you have your Christmas tree yet?" they called.

"No, you haven't, have you?" They answered themselves as they peered in at the open door. "Well, here's a dandy, just the right height. We put a base on it too."

Carefully they carried in a lovely little fir tree, tiny cones hanging to the branches. It was fresh from the mountains nearby, and its pungent aroma scented the whole room. I tried to pay them, but they laughingly refused and left.

It was fun to trim the tree. Each little ornament was talked about, its history explained. Jimmy broke one silver ball and Joanie tripped and fell against the tree, almost upsetting it, but they "helped." Together we went to the store, scuffing through the soft snow, to buy Christmas lights—our first ones.

Toward evening I left long enough to run next door to engage a girl for the next morning to stay with the children while I went across the river to the church to play for an early Sunday morning Christmas service. When I came back, the cheerful lights of my home filled me with joy. I stamped off the snow before coming in the door. Christmas Eve! Beverly was excited about Santa Claus. She helped the older twins hang their stockings on the back of the davenport. She hung her own and one for Jimmy and Joan. We sang a few carols, Beverly holding the fat red candle so that I could see to play the piano; all the lights were turned out except the little ones on the Christmas tree. I read the story of the Christ child from the book of Luke,

Beverly trying not to drip candle wax on my book. The children protested that they were not sleepy, but soon I was putting them into bed, first Jimmy and Joan, each in a small bed with sides that fastened up. Joanie could say a little prayer, but Jimmy left out most of the words of his prayer. The older twins undressed themselves and got into their sleepers. Helping them into their big bed after hearing them say their prayers, I kissed them as I assured them, "Yes, Santa will be here soon," "No, he won't have trouble finding our house," "Yes, I know we did not live here last year, but Santa will know."

Then I noticed Beverly scratching her arms. "Beverly, why aren't you getting your pajamas on?"

"I itch and my head hurts and I don't feel good." Her face puckered up and she tried hard not to cry.

"Beverly, dear, come here to me." I held her close a minute, then looked at her bare arms. Why hadn't I noticed before? Her soft skin was broken here and there by small red eruptions. Hurriedly undressing her, I found more marks on her body. Chicken pox! We had had a few cases at school. I explained to Beverly what I thought it was, calmed her by telling her that the spots would disappear as they had on Anne, the little neighbor girl. Helping her undress, I talked to her of Christmas morning, tucked her into bed, kissed her, and turned out the lights. At the door I stood awhile, listening for their quiet breathing, then went into the living room.

All of my iron self-discipline seemed to be slipping away. As I walked slowly into the living room, tears came into my eyes—tears of self-pity, of hopelessness, of despair, of loneliness. It was not fair—it could not be just! What could I do now? How would I be able to get a housekeeper? Without one I could not teach—could not support my family. I was sobbing in emotional desperation. Now I would be tied to this house the whole two weeks of vacation with a chicken-pox quarantine. I just couldn't do it. No trip to the valley! No adult to talk with the whole two weeks. All strangers around me. Why had I taken this job of teaching in a lonely mountain town sixty miles from the people I knew? Yes, it was the only vacancy in my field of teaching, and of course I had to make a living. "But I can't do it alone," I said—first to myself and then aloud.

In despair I dropped to my knees and bowed my head. I was crying unrestrainedly. Then my eyes were drawn to the only light in the room, the Christmas tree bulbs, the tiny bulb in the star shining on the top of the tree. The little glow of that light seemed to become brighter; it seemed to take on a significance. Almost as if someone had spoken I heard these words: "You are not alone. I am always with you. Do not be afraid."

The words penetrated my consciousness, my mind, and my heart. What did I have to cry about? My selfish fears, my worries, troubles, dropped away from me and I was filled with a peace that "surpasseth understanding."

The tears dried on my cheeks, leaving a wrinkled, tight feeling. My heart overflowed with thanksgiving to God for the blessing of health, for the ability to earn a living for my children, and for our love for one another. What a marvelous opportunity I had of proving my worth! What did I have to fear? With God's help—of course I could do it!

By the last weekend of the vacation, the children were well enough for me to go to the valley to find a housekeeper. Anna had been busy inquiring about. Just before I arrived she had persuaded Madeline to quit her present job and come with me. The children were overjoyed to see her again.

CHAPTER TWENTY-TWO

It was late that Saturday morning in January before the sun rose over the jagged mountain peaks and touched our little town. Long before sunrise, the bustle in our house warned of excitement.

"And Mommy, can Margie and me wear our new corduroy suits you made us for Christmas?"

My voice was muffled, from the depths of the one real clothes closet, as I answered an affirmative.

"Beverly, here's yours too. Hurry so you can help me with Jim and Joan."

"Mommy, can we get the new shoes today?"

"Uh-huh, we've saved five shoe stamps, and I've plenty of gas rationing stamps."

"And we are going to church, to our own little white church in Bozeman?" Beverly, ever the more serious one, missed the ties of the life we had lived before.

"Joanie's trying to put on her skirt, and she's got it backward. This way, Joan, turn it around so you can see the little flowers of embroidery on the front."

My thoughts raced as I pulled on snowsuits, buttoned and zipped.

"Beverly, see that everyone has on overshoes and mittens. I'll get the car out of the garage and fill the radiator with hot water. Hope it isn't too hard to start." My last words were lost as I picked up the pail and teakettle of boiling water and hurried out the back door.

The cold air felt good. The snow underfoot did not crunch as it did when the thermometer was below zero. A beautiful day to drive to the valley! The snow plows had kept the highways clear and there had been no new snow now for several days.

I opened the garage door and went around to the front of the car. Reaching under the hood I tightened the petcock on the base of the radiator and slowly poured in the hot water. Earlier in the morning I had put a big ash pan of red hot clinkers from the furnace under the oil pan of the car. The garage was narrow and I bumped my elbow a sharp crack when I pulled back after touching the still-hot pan.

With a few coughs and false starts the engine roared, and I pushed the choke partway in. Keeping the motor racing, I backed out of the garage and drove around to the front of the house. The door opened and the five children came tumbling out and down the steps. Jim slowly brought up the rear, sitting down on each step and bumping and scooting himself on down.

Going back into the house, I started to pick up my pocketbook and then decided to take a last look at the furnace. I ran down the stairs, throwing the lock on the back door as I paused on the back entry landing. The basement was warm and dark. A strong scent of coal and ashes, of potatoes in the bin gave me a sense of security—of food and warmth. Pulling on an old pair of the children's father's leather gloves, I opened the furnace door and threw in several large chunks of coal. A careful look at dampers and drafts and I was running up the steps and through the kitchen. The sun reflected on the shiny flowered oilcloth on the kitchen table.

On through the living room I went picking up a folded blanket from the davenport. Again I took the pocketbook, found the keys to the house. I looked around at the empty rooms. How quiet it seemed without the five eager, chattering children! It seemed almost strange in there. The old piano drew my eyes. My husband had traded a milk cow for that a month after he had taken me to the ranch as a bride. I paused a moment.

"Mommy, Mommy, are you coming?"

"Hurry up, Mommy!"

The motor of the car sounded good to me. It was fun to be driving to the valley—to be seeing friends, to be going to some larger stores. The hard-surface road was dry. Snow piled on each side made me thankful for the big rotary plows that had chopped up the drifts and thrown the snow out to the edge of the road.

We climbed steadily until we came to the mountain pass that we called the Hill. The sun glanced from the thousands of snow crystals, reflected from the shiny wires of the powerful electric lines that marched with measured steps around the side of the mountain and disappeared into the canyon where the dam and falls gave them their power.

The sight of a few cars on the road filled me with confidence that other people thought the weather was going to be good for the weekend. The last final climb of the pass made me shift the car into a lower gear. As we dropped over the top, we caught a view of the Bridger Range of mountains—home for us. I raised a mittened hand and pointed at a distant peak.

"Look, children, there's Old Baldy."

"Can we see the M on it?"

"'Course not, silly, we're too far away," Beverly explained. "Besides, it's all covered with snow."

The car ate up the miles. We were happy to be out—the first time in almost two months. In another hour we turned off the road and into a driveway.

"Auntie Anna's house," chorused the children.

"They're home. I can see the pickup," I said, more to myself than to them.

My sister-in-law had no children of her own and loved my little orphans as completely as I could wish. She was out of the door before the motor had stopped.

"My, you're early birds. Get out and come in." She shaded her eyes with one hand as she wiped the other on her apron.

"There's Bo, Marilyn. Here, Bo, here, Bo," Margie called as the big cow dog ran barking to our car.

Beverly cranked down the window and the shaggy dog reached up to the car and tried to lick the eager faces.

"Aren't you coming in?" called Joe, my brother-in-law, as he came from the cow barn, carrying two buckets of foaming milk.

"No, we'll be back here by evening. Wanted to be sure you'd put another potato in the kettle for supper. Got to buy shoes for my brood. They're practically barefoot. Want anything in town?"

"Nope. We went there yesterday. Bought everything we could afford. Oh, say, pick up our mail on your way back," Anna said and backed away and waved us on.

I turned the car around in the yard and started on toward Bozeman. The children still leaned out of the windows waving and calling, "Good-bye, Auntie Anna. Good-bye, Uncle Joe. Good-bye, Bo."

"Close the windows and sit back on the seat," I called. The heater on our old car was never very efficient.

"This window's stuck, Mother," Beverly explained. "I can't make it work."

"Let me try," offered Marilyn.

I stopped the car and leaned over the seat to crank the stubborn window closed.

126

"I'm hungry," Jimmy said.

From near my feet, I took the brown paper sack and began to dole out oatmeal cookies.

"Beverly, there's a sack of apples up above the back seat. Just one for each person, now, honey. We'll want some later on."

Eating is such an entertaining experience for children tired of riding. Crumbs were no worry in our old car, and we ate and crunched happily.

The day ran by on happy feet. Familiar voices, familiar faces, the warmth of friendship and love—these made living worthwhile! In no time at all it was Sunday afternoon, and I kept looking at my watch.

"It's two o'clock. I must go. I'm lucky the weather is so beautiful. Come on, kids. Let's get those snowsuits on. We must get home before dark."

And how the sun shone on us as we drove back onto the highway! Jim leaned his red helmeted head toward me, and Joan's head was on him. Their warm bodies sagged in sleep against me. Their little white overshoes stuck straight out over the edge of the car seat. It was quiet in the back of the car too. So much unaccustomed excitement for two days! They were all relaxed and sleepy.

The first twenty miles were gone before we ran into the snow. Big heavy flakes, not much wind! I looked up to the south toward the pass. Yes, it was snowing hard up there. First there were just little swirls of snow on the highway. But in a few miles the wind began to drive the snow against the windshield. The wipers could hardly keep it clear. My heart in my throat, I drove carefully but as fast as was safe. "Hurry! Hurry to that big hill before the going gets too tough!" I urged myself on. Snow was piling up on the sides of the road by the time we started the real climb up toward the pass. If I could keep the car moving fast—but there were turns and switchbacks near the top— no possibility of any speed, especially with those drifts on the edges of the road. Now there was more snow on the road, and the climbing was steeper. I shifted to second gear. We were near the top, but I was already "lugging" the motor. I had to change to low—no good in the snow. The wheels spun—we slowed, and then stopped. I was stuck. It was that bad west corner near the top.

I sat for a second, trying to collect my terrified thoughts. No snowplow would come over this road until tomorrow morning, I knew. It was becoming bitter cold. I dared not get out, leave the children, and walk for help. It was miles and miles to the nearest house that I knew of. I could not take the children with me, couldn't carry them all, too far for the littlest ones to walk all the way. They could not be left here alone. That was too dangerous.

"Mommy, what are we stopping for? Are we home? I'm getting cold." The children had all roused. As carefully as I tried to control my voice, some of the emotion was transferred to their wakening minds.

"Now, Beverly," I said briskly, "wrap that blanket around you three girls, and I'll tuck one around Jim and Joan. I'm going to try to shovel us out. There are some more apples and cookies if you're hungry." But I hadn't fooled them. Their big eyes stared at me, and they were very quiet.

Every good Montana driver carries a shovel in the trunk of his car. I wielded mine busily for a while, digging out the snow under and ahead of the wheels, making a free track before me. Shielding my face from the sharp cold, I tried to keep my back to the wind. I got into the car and tried to back a little and then pull ahead. But the grade was too steep, and I was losing rather than gaining ground. I tried to shovel again. I straightened up to ease my aching back muscles and looked wearily off up the mountain. Stories I had read of people freezing to death in their cars raced through my mind. A few actual cases I had known myself. Asphyxiation from monoxide poisoning was a danger if I kept the engine going. One of my school students had died that way.

I shuddered and had begun to shovel again when I saw a man with a shovel over his shoulder coming across the snow. He climbed through the fence and came nearer.

"Need some help?" he asked. He was a complete stranger, and there was not a building in sight.

I nodded. He looked us over, noticed the children in the car, and began to shovel, scooping up big bites of snow and throwing them off the road. I shoveled too, but my loads were just nibbles compared to his. We didn't talk— just worked. I didn't even think of asking him who he was. I didn't care. It would have been trivial in a time like that.

After a while he stopped and walked around the car. He said slowly, "Let's try it. You drive, and I'll push."

"If it goes, I'll keep right on. So I'll say thank you now, because I won't be able to stop and start again."

He nodded. "Start very slowly. Don't let those wheels begin to spin," he called as I opened the car door, got in, and started the engine.

I could feel him put his shoulder to the back fender. The car moved slowly forward. I dared not turn around even to wave. Cautiously I kept an even pressure on the accelerator. We went on slowly to the top and over the pass. The wind was not so strong on this side of the hill, and there was less snow.

Beverly leaned over my shoulder. "Mommy, who was it? Who helped us?"

"I don't know," I said wonderingly.

"He's like the Good Samaritan in the Bible, I think."

Without any more trouble, we went on home.

Weeks later I came over this pass again. I looked carefully across the hills on both sides trying to see any sign of a house or any form of habitation. There was none. I knew it was used only for summer pasture for cattle which were always taken to the valleys for the winter.

I looked again and again every time I drove over this road. Often I wondered who came to help me. It didn't really matter. I needed help, and help came to me.

CHAPTER TWENTY-THREE

With the closing of school in May we began to make plans to "fold our tents" and move back down to the valley, at least for the summer. The school board gave me a contract for the next year. I was grateful for the kind offer but asked permission to consider before signing it. In two weeks I would give my answer. If I could find a position in a high school in a town in the valley, it would be better for me because it was so hard to keep a housekeeper up there away from the larger towns.

On the way to Manhattan, with my brood of five children beside me and behind us the truck with our furniture, I took stock of my situation. My last month's paycheck, folded and lying in my pocketbook, would have to do for all the three months' summer expenses and for the month of September—until I was paid again. Not much for six of us! Should I try to get a job—if I could find one—for the summer and leave the children with a housekeeper? No, that would defeat my purpose—that of rearing my own children! Ways to implement that single paycheck must be devised.

Our house in Manhattan had been rented just for the school year. It had been venture. The people who had lived there had moved out a month before the end of school and had not paid the last two months' rent.

About the middle of May I had made a trip to Manhattan on a Saturday to spade and plant the early garden in the large yard back of our house. Raising vegetables meant food for our living. At least four hundred quarts was the minimum that I put on the shelves each year. I canned everything I could raise or afford to buy. If a friend had apples that could be had for the picking, I filled a shelf with apple-sauce. Tomatoes I could not ripen in Montana's short season, at least not enough for canning. But we raised many; they were large and beginning to change color by September, and we carefully packed them in boxes. As they ripened, we canned at least fifty quarts of them.

The wild chokecherries were another source for filling my shelves. One afternoon spent picking them, several days of cooking and squeezing the juice through a clean white cloth, and we had plenty of juice for jelly for the year. Carrots would keep, packed in sand, for the whole winter; big heads of cabbage we hung in the cool root cellar. A large bin was always filled with potatoes. The odors of that part of the basement were redolent but spoke to me of many meals for my family.

All of these the children would help me do. We could work together. The three older girls would help me plant the remainder of the garden. I had taught them to walk along in the rows that I had made, drop two kernels of corn, step one foot in the row and then the other one right in front of that one and drop two more kernels. Barefooted, they liked to push the soft earth to cover the seed. We made a game out of our work. The rows planted, we usually sat awhile on the grass with Jimmy and Joan and told stories.

Carefully cataloging these items in my mind as we rode along, I probed for another idea for adding to that one small paycheck. Milk cost so much for six of us! Always when we had lived in the little log house I had kept a cow at Crowalls' and milked her night and morning. Now that cow had been sold.

The old truck's bumping gently into our front porch railing put an end to my puzzling. As we unloaded everything, the children ran happily back and forth, carrying toys, clothes, light boxes, renewing acquaintance with the rooms, the stairs, the bannister to slide on, the door that opened out on a long back stairs leading to the backyard. Taking their kitty to the old barn, they continued to explore familiar places. They remembered the hole down under the back steps where they could dig. They were at home and at peace.

But the next morning my problem was still nagging at my consciousness as we set the house in order. If I only had someone to talk it over with!

"Mother," Beverly called, "where are you?" She came running through the hall to the kitchen where I was putting away pans and unpacking dishes.

"Here," I answered from my squatting position beside a basket of packed utensils.

"Hurry, Mother. Someone wants you on the phone over at the Chaldens' house."

I hurried.

"Hello, Elsie." Through the receiver I recognized Alden Crowall's slow drawl. "Say, I heard you got back yesterday. Thought you might want to know that heifer of yours freshened the other day. Looks like she'd give enough milk for the calf and your family too—big bag full. You want to find a place to keep her there at the edge of town? I'll bring her in to you."

"Sure, Alden, and thanks!" I said it confidently, but I did not feel confident at all. That heifer—cow, I suppose I should call her—was a wild little range animal. She'd be tough to break. When the cowboys wanted to milk a range cow, they would run it in the chute and milk it that way. I could not do that here.

Nevertheless, here was an answer to one problem—if I had the backbone to accept the challenge.

Down the road about a quarter of a mile lived the Roberts

on the edge of town. They kept a few cows in a pasture. I thought of them and the wheels of my mind began to spin. Always when a problem bothered me I felt so much better if I could tackle it physically as well as mentally. Helping Jim and Joan into the little red wagon, with Margie and Marilyn pushing from behind and Beverly solemnly plodding along beside me in the dusty road, I headed for the Roberts' place. The sun was bright; my mind felt lighter; the mountains before and beyond me gave me their old familiar strength and assurance. To the children it was an adventure—nothing to be feared—something to be anticipated. I talked to them of the cow and the little calf, of the milk we would have.

As we neared the Roberts' yard I felt a knot of fear tighten my chest and quicken my breathing. "Suppose they won't let me keep the cow here?" I asked myself. "Always a coward," I answered, and set my teeth tightly together as I pushed open the gate. The friendliness of Mrs. Robert and her husband and their acceptance of my plan brought quick relief. My steps were light as I pulled the little wagon back up the road.

The cow and the calf arrived the next day. The heifer made a pass at Mr. Robert with her horns as he helped unload her and drove her into the pasture with his cows. Her calf was put in a little enclosure near the corral by the barn. Mr. Robert shook his head as he turned to me.

"You think you can milk that ornery critter there, Mrs. Doig?" He leaned on the top rail of the corral and waited for my answer.

"I *have* to," I said. "You have a pair of kickers, don't you?"

"Got 'em somewhere. I'll look 'em up before evening."

Big-eyed, the children—standing on the outside of the

corral—had watched the unloading. Now they tried to get their hands on the little calf. With a bawl he flipped his tail and ran to the opposite side of the pen. Calling to them, I started back up the road, mentally shaking my head too.

About sundown we went down there again, with a milk pail. Mr. Robert drove my cow into the small corral and somehow we managed to get a rope fastened to the halter that had been put on her. We tied her to a roping post. By letting the calf in and getting him to begin sucking on the left side of the cow, we got her quieted enough for us to fasten the kickers on her hind legs. I picked up the pail and attempted to take hold of the two teats on the right side of the cow. When she felt my touch, her forward lunge almost knocked her off her feet. Again I took hold of the teats and this time milked a few streams before she tried to reach me with her head. Her tail slashed my face wickedly.

Then the calf gave a mighty bunt on her bag, and the cow kicked—even with the kickers on—with such force that she knocked me off my balance. I landed on the ground with her hoof in my milk pail. Hurrying to the pump to wash it, I came back and tried to get hold of the teats again. By this time the calf had sucked most of the milk from his side of the udder and now began to nuzzle his slobbery mouth toward the teats I was trying so hard to squeeze.

"No fair sucking my half of the milk," I yelled and pushed the calf's head aside. I squatted on a milk stool and put the pail between my knees. Just then the calf bunted his empty side of the udder. The cow lunged again; I jumped out of her way and spilled the milk in my pail. I returned to get just a few strippings of milk in the bucket, which I handed over the corral to Beverly.

I gave the cow some ground grain. At first she sniffed and blew, then began to eat it, stopping often to glare at me with rolling eyes. Taking the calf by the ear and twisting sharply on his tail, I pushed and pulled him away from his mother and into the little calf pasture. Mr. Robert loosened the rope off the cow.

"Look out," he yelled. "Here she comes."

I opened the gate leading to the cow pasture and got out of the way—quick!

"Wow!" I said as I picked up the almost empty bucket. "Better luck next time!"

Mr. Robert shook his head. "She's a wild one. Don't think you'll ever gentle her."

"Well, I'll be here in the morning again. What time do you milk?"

"'Round six o'clock. I'll help you get the kickers again. Try giving her the grain first this time. Now she's got a taste of it, it may help."

We tried everything. That mean little heifer never did become tame. I had to tie her up each time, put the kickers on her, and still she gave me plenty of trouble. She was as determined as I was. But by now it was a matter of principle with me, as well as economics.

The battle was repeated each night and morning all summer. Sometimes she managed to spill all the milk just as I was about through milking her, but usually I got about four quarts a milking. When I could sit on the milking stool, I held the pail between my knees, but often she wouldn't stand still long enough for me to do this.

The calf grew rapidly and greedily snatched at the teats on my side as well as on his own. His teeth were sharp. His wet mouth made my hands slippery. Getting him out of the corral was more of a challenge each time as he became bigger and stronger. Grabbing his right ear with my right hand, his tail with my left, I pulled, tugged, and tail-twisted until I worried him to the little gate that Beverly held open for me after I had finished milking.

Perhaps the battle was good for me; maybe I released all my antagonisms on this calf and cow. Every time I felt somewhat triumphant, though exhausted, as I pulled the little wagon with one hand and carried the milk pail in the other and plodded back home.

But we had milk—plenty of it. And we had cream—enough to make our own butter. From the sour milk we made cottage cheese and fed the whey to the hens we kept in the chicken yard.

When school began that fall we sent the cow and calf back to the Crowalls' ranch. As she was loaded into the truck she kicked viciously. Over the edge of the truck rack she shook her head at me and snorted angrily.

In December Alden had the fat calf butchered and the meat put into a locker for me. As we ate the meat that winter I enjoyed each bite.

CHAPTER TWENTY-FOUR

We had been in Manhattan less than a week that summer when I had a sudden hunch. Why not drive to Three Forks, a town just twelve miles away, and check on the school vacancies? Helping the children wash their faces and put on clean clothes, I packed them all into the car and drove down to the historic little town where the three forks of the Missouri River join. As we rode along, I told the children about Lewis and Clark, pointing to the Gallatin River on our right, explaining the reason for the name of the Madison River, showing them the Jefferson River winding its way along the hills to the west. The stories of Sacajawea and her little papoose on her back and the one of John Colter and his run for his life held their interest until we reached the center of the little town. We stopped by a large bronze monument. Three big trees in a fenced-in area stood for the three rivers.

It took us only a few minutes to find the house of the school superintendent, Mr. Sorenson.

"Mr. Sorenson is up the street in his office in the school building," his wife told me as she came to the door in answer to my knock. She pointed toward a large brick building about ten blocks away.

As I parked at the schoolhouse, we saw the swings and teeter-totters around behind the building. I pointed them out to the children.

"Why don't you go swing while I talk to Mr. Sorenson? Beverly and Margie and Marilyn, you can take turns pushing Jimmy and Joan." The words were hardly out of my mouth before the girls were helping the younger twins to tumble from the car and hurry across the grass. Hearing the chattering voices, a custodian came around the corner of the building, hose and sprinkler in his hands.

"Is it okay for my children to use the swings?" I called to him.

He nodded. "Sure thing!" he said and went on trailing hose across the lawn.

I went up the steps and into the building. Something inside me said, "This is it." Following the sound of the clicking of a typewriter, I went into the open door on my left. A broad-shouldered man with black hair in loose ringlets lifted his head and looked straight at me. His eyes were as black as his hair and very penetrating.

I'd hate to be caught doing something bad and have him look at me, I thought as I stood in the doorway.

Then he smiled and said, "Is there anything I can do for you?"

"Yes, I'm looking for a vacancy in an English department. Can you help me?"

For a moment he looked at me steadily. Then he asked curtly, "How did you know?"

"Know what?" I countered, puzzled.

"That we need an English teacher here? The draft just took our high school English man," he said. "What are your qualifications?"

We got busy on credits, transcripts, majors, minors, names for recommendations. He asked me where I had taught before, how many years of experience I had had, why I wanted to come to Three Forks. At last he said, "What was your salary last year?"

"Sixteen hundred, but they promised me seventeen hundred if I could come back."

This was 1943. The wartime squeeze was just beginning

to take hold. People were finding good-salaried jobs in munitions plants and airplane factories. There was no longer such a superfluity of teachers.

"If your recommendations prove satisfactory, I can offer you eighteen hundred," he promised me. "I'll let you know in a few days."

I thanked him and left the building, walking on air. Why I was so sure of getting the job I don't know, but I was. Two days later the doorbell rang at our house. When I opened the door, there stood Mrs. Sorenson with a contract for me in her hand.

Months later I found out that Mr. Sorenson had called my former superintendent and been satisfied with the answer given about my qualifications as a teacher. When I heard what had been said, I was much disturbed: "Mrs. Doig makes up in enthusiasm, interest, and good hard work whatever she may lack in experience and training in high school teaching."

My ego was dreadfully deflated. What a poor recommendation that seemed to me!

Over the years I have gradually learned to value that statement which got me a much-needed job so I could continue to earn a living for my children and me.

CHAPTER TWENTY-FIVE

The summer in Manhattan was a happy one. I hoed in the garden, canned the colorful vegetables, sewed for the children; they played on the lawn, never beyond the sound of my voice. Margie fell in love for the first time. It was shortly after the older twins' fifth birthday that I discovered it.

A little boy named Teddie lived down at the end of the block. His blond hair was sun-bleached almost white, and his eyes were as blue as the wild flax flowers. He was shy, seldom speaking in my presence. But he played with the children hour after hour.

One evening I heard voices outside my open bedroom window. I stopped the sewing machine and listened.

"But you're my g-girl, aren't y-you?" Teddy stammered softly.

"But I don't want you to kiss me." It was Margie's voice. She spoke quite distinctly.

"If you're my g-girl, I should k-kiss you," he insisted. "Besides you can't come over to my d-daddy's b-beehouse and have honey any more if you aren't my g-girl."

"Oh, all right, hurry up and kiss me."

There was no sound for a few minutes.

"Now, let's go get some honey." I looked up to see them scampering away hand in hand.

But Margie's little friend was not the only one who showed signs of amorous intentions that summer.

During the months of July and August my brother's wife, Alma, came to visit us, bringing her six-month-old baby with her. What fun we had playing with Lois Jean! Never had we had a "new" baby because the children had all been babies at the same time. We'd never been able to say, "The baby." Since Beverly, there had been two babies each time. Lois Jean was a new experience to us.

My brother had returned from the New Guinea campaign of World War II and was in pilot's training in an Air Force base. Housing was so difficult near where he was stationed that Alma could be with him very little, so she had come to visit us.

She helped me with my sewing. Always during the summer I made the children's clothes for the whole year. Dresses for four little girls, shirts and often overalls too for one boy took much sewing. Alma made such good button-holes, had such artistic taste about touches of trimming. Time went by swiftly. Adult companionship was something I had missed much since Jim's death; I savored every minute of the time.

Never having had time or money for social life, I had had to be satisfied with working long hours, not giving myself time to brood or think. We had no telephone. The little radio was seldom turned on. After the children were in bed, if I felt lonely, I would go to the piano and, looking up at Jim's picture, play and sing to him. I tried not to think about the future. Alma's being there was good for all of us.

Sometime about the first of August, on a warm Saturday night, we all sat in the living room as I read the evening story. A short ring of the doorbell broke off our story in the middle of a sentence. With book in hand, I went to the open door.

Standing outside the screen was a very good-looking man. From the top of his gray Stetson to the tip of his polished shoes, he was carefully dressed. He smiled and his blue eyes lighted up.

"No, you don't know me, but I'm Bert Hartnell," he said all in one breath, then paused a moment. "Do you have a barn?"

"Why, yes, I have a barn," I answered dumbly.

"Can I buy it?" he asked quickly.

"Er—oh, I don't see how you could use it. It sits on the back of our lot here. We use part of it for a garage and part for a chicken house." My mind was still so surprised it hadn't moved out of low gear.

"No," I said at last, "I don't want to sell it."

"May I come in?" the stranger then asked.

"Of course, come in." My sense of western hospitality finally reached the surface, but my surprise must have bristled out all over me.

Taking off his hat, he stepped into the hall and followed me into the living room. His hair was fair to match his blue eyes. Little damp curls showed where his hat had been on his forehead. He brushed them back with his arm.

I introduced him to Alma, recited the names of each of the children and asked him to sit. He did—evidently at ease. He talked of people whom we both knew and told me where he lived with his parents on a ranch near town.

Joan crawled onto my lap and leaned sleepily against me. Jimmy's eyes were closed as he laid his head back on the davenport.

"You'll have to excuse me, but I must put these children to bed," I said.

"I'll help," Alma offered quickly. We went up the stairs.

"That's all right. I'll wait here," he called up to us.

Wait? Wait for what? I wondered.

Taking longer than usual, we puttered over the children's prayers, picking up their clothes and laying them on chairs. But when we came downstairs, there was Bert Hartnell. He stayed and stayed. We talked. Unused to late hours as Alma and I were, we yawned and fidgeted. At last he rose, said good-night, and drove away.

"Well, whatever that was—that's that!" I said to Alma as we wearily climbed the stairs.

But it wasn't. Next Saturday he came again. This time he had some candy for the children. They were so very shy of male creatures that they would not come near him nor let him approach them. Finally he put the candy on the stairsteps, left it there, and came into the living room to talk.

That night I outdid myself—telling what a meanie I had been in my teens, how I had flirted with the boys, broken their hearts, collected them like scalps to my belt. Oh, I had a very good time trying to scare him away.

When he left at about midnight I mentally dusted off my hands. "That's the last we'll see of him, I promise you." I laughed as Alma and I stumbled off to bed.

Next Saturday it was right after supper that he came. In one hand was a sack of gumdrops for the children. In the other he held a big brown paper sack. He came into the kitchen where I was finishing the dishes and set the big sack on the table.

"Like corn on the cob?" he asked joyfully as he pulled out ear after ear of golden corn, husked and ready for the pot. "How about fried chicken?" He reached into the sack and brought out a plastic bag with chickens cut up ready for frying.

"Here's how I figure it," he went on. "We could fry the chicken tonight and go on a picnic tomorrow, right after church. Where would you like to go?"

"I'd like to go back to our ranch, away up in the mountains," said Beverly who had come into the room and stood looking up at him.

"That's where we'll go. Can you tell me the way?" He looked down into her serious eyes.

She nodded. "Away up there," and she pointed to the north.

"How about it, everybody? Agreed?"

We still stood dumbfounded. Alma found her voice first. "Won't that be fun?"

I nodded.

"Shall we get at that chicken frying?" He walked toward the stove.

His spark of enthusiasm caught the interest of everyone. The children became excited and almost friendly. Margie and Marilyn ventured close enough to look up at him and listen to his eager planning.

He did not stay late that night but arrived next morning soon after we had returned from Sunday school. We took baskets of food, blankets, and a big jug of cold water. Scrambling into the car I counted—one, two . . . nine. But all were children except the three, so we took just one car.

As we drove across the valley and up Dry Creek, we pointed out landmarks. Reaching the little schoolhouse where I had taught for three years, we turned off toward the mountains to the west and climbed steadily till we saw the ranch house ahead of us. Memories flooded over me, and I felt sick and hurt. I turned my face away and looked off up to the mountains for a moment of control. I had not been back up here for almost three years. Nothing had changed except for some replacements of freshly peeled logs in the big corral.

"Where shall we picnic? The Allens have the ranch now, don't they? They won't care, will they?" Bert's voice brought me back quickly.

"No, it'll be all right. Let's go up in the horse pasture

a ways. There's a little spring and a clump of serviceberries that may be ripe." I directed to the left, got out and opened the gate when he stopped, and closed it after he had driven through.

We picked a good spot, and the children tumbled from the car and took off in all directions. Bert spread a blanket for Alma and the baby, and then another on which he placed the lunch.

I looked about me. It is curious how an old wound that should be healed can throb upon certain stimulations, I thought, and absently tried to help Bert. He seemed to sense my mood and didn't talk. The children ran back and forth, bringing us flowers and little cones from the pine trees.

When the lunch had been spread out, Bert rounded up the children. They ate hungrily, and he waited on them. How familiar it was to have a man waiting on the children and yet how strange—yet how could it seem familiar when it had been so long!

The children fed and off to run and chatter, Alma and I and Bert leaned back on the blankets and looked up at the blue, blue sky. It was so quiet. I sorted out each sound and sight. Occasionally a light breeze set the pine needles humming. A big chicken hawk screamed overhead and was gone. The distant tinkle of a milk cow's bell let us know that we were not alone in the pasture. All of this was like a familiar arm around my waist, a well-known voice in my ear.

"Alma and the baby have gone to sleep," I said at last.

"Uh-huh," Bert said as he reached his arm over the edge of the blanket and pulled a blade of grass and chewed on it. "You reckon there's danger of wood ticks for the kids?"

"Oh, I'll look them over carefully," I said, "when I give

them their baths tonight. I don't worry much about ticks."

"Did you like to live up here?" he asked.

"Yes, I did." I did not trust myself to say more. No one wants to hear of others' sorrows. I had learned that the hard way, those first hurting months of grief.

At last I said, "It's so peaceful here. It's hard to realize that a horrible war is tearing at the world's vitals."

It was a quiet afternoon, a restful time. We were reluctant to leave. That evening after he had gone and the children were asleep, Alma and I sat awhile on the front porch in the deepening twilight.

"Is he coming to see you or me?" I asked suddenly. "Why does he come?"

"I'm sure it's you." Alma pushed it on me.

"But why?" I asked. "What can he get from all this? What does he expect? I'll tell you what, Alma. We'll know after next week. If he comes while I'm gone to Deer Lodge to attend conference, we'll know it's you."

Alma took care of the children, and I drove the old Chevy over the continental divide to Butte and on up the valley to Deer Lodge. I was gone a week. When I returned and drove up in front of our yard, about sunset, my brood fell upon me, asking me questions, telling me of little happenings. The care of my five often seemed a heavy burden, but to see them again after this absence warmed all the corners of my heart.

It was difficult to walk with the children clustered all about me. Awkwardly I picked up Jim and Joan in my arms, and the three girls followed close at my heels as we went up the steps. Snatches of their words reached my consciousness.

"And I found her first."

"Well, I saw the little kittens first."

"One's black. He's mine. I named him Blackie."

"She's way back in the old hay, Mother. You'd think she'd be hot there," Beverly observed in her adult-like way.

A horn sounded as we came up the porch steps, and we turned to see Bert's blue car come to a stop by the walk.

"Hi, there! Have a good time?" And he was up the walk and holding the screen door open for me.

My surprise must have been obvious, for he laughed and said, "You didn't beat me much, did you?"

We skipped the evening story and hurried to their prayers that night, for there were so many things to tell them—what I had done, whom I had seen—and they told me all about the old cat and her kittens. Later coming downstairs slowly, I looked into the living room at Bert and Alma. I must bring this thing to a head.

"Bert, shall we go out on the porch and talk?" I suggested.

Alma looked at me knowingly and said, "Mind if I go to bed? You two carry on."

We sat in the porch swing, not talking for a few minutes, as we began a rhythm of push—wait—push the swing.

"Bert," I began abruptly, "why are you coming to see us?"

"Because I want to marry you," he answered quickly. "Is there any reason why I can't? It's been three years since Jim died. Would he have cared?"

I know I must have been silent for a few minutes—stunned into silence—me, the garrulous one. "Oh, I don't know," I answered rather jerkily. "But, Bert, I have no desire at all to get married. And anyway, any man marrying me would get only half a person. Half of me is dead. I can't build it back. No one can."

I stopped. His head had dropped as I talked. "May I try?" he asked, at last.

He continued to come to see us. He was so good to us and for us. When we moved to Three Forks for school that fall, he helped us in numerous ways. I had often laughingly exclaimed, "I should hire a male creature for a few hours each week and pay him so that the children wouldn't be so shy of men and big boys." Perhaps this would do the trick.

But the children never accepted Bert. When he talked to them about having him as a father, they would say, "We don't want you to marry us."

He tried always to become friends with them. At Christmastime he bought each one a carefully chosen gift. But never once did they really make up to him—they only tolerated him. Probably it was my fault; unconsciously I had kept their father alive in their hearts.

One night Bert scolded us thoroughly. We told him, for fun, of the police warning we had had the night before. A railroad bum had been troubling residents, and the police had followed his tracks to our front porch, looked at his footprints in the fresh snow on the front porch where he had stood by the window, then followed his tracks until they had caught him. They came to our house and gave us a severe warning that we should lock our house, front and back, at night. Bert was alarmed; his concern for us was real.

But the idea of marrying was still repugnant to me. I told him how I felt. He was sure he could change my mind.

One day after school was out in the spring the children came bringing in the mail. A letter from my sister set me all agog. She was going to be married in June. Would I be able to sing for her wedding?

A few days later a letter from one of my brothers was more surprising. From it fell a check for more than the amount necessary to buy train tickets for the children and me to go to the wedding. I shied away from any kind of charity, but somehow—in my foolish feminine reasoning—this did not smack of charity. Pocketing my pride, I wrote a hurried note to my brother and packed our one suitcase and two boxes and we were off for Warrensburg.

We returned two weeks later, glad to be home. The pansies by the front door lifted lovely face-blossoms to us. The air seemed deliciously cool after the warm, humid climate of Missouri. We unlocked the door, took the mail from the box, and went into the cool, darkened hall.

Sorting personal letters from advertisements and bills, I quickly tore open a letter marked with an APO. My youngest brother, stationed in Italy, was a navigator on a B-24. I read of his successful bombing expedition. "Still going after our thirteenth mission," he wrote jokingly.

"Mommy, can I burn this letter from Bert Hartnell?" Margie waved it in the air.

"Yes, yes," I said absently, not listening, trying to get rid of her for a few minutes.

Avidly I read the long, interesting details of my brother's experiences in the little Italian towns. "The churches dominate the landscape," he wrote, "as they actually do the lives of the people." Tremulously, I read the cheerful closing.

Then I turned to the other mail.

"Margie, where's that letter from Bert Hartnell?"

"Oh, I burned it," she said matter-of-factly.

"What!" I yelped.

"That's what you said I could do, Mother, wasn't it?"

The consternation in my expression must have disturbed her, for she came to me and we went to the kitchen where she pointed to the charred pages in the empty cookstove grate. But I was not unhappy about it, really.

That was the last we ever heard of Bert Hartnell for years. What did he say in the letter? I never did find out.

CHAPTER TWENTY-SIX

Jimmy was three years old when we moved into the little brown house in Three Forks. The arrangement of the house was unusual. The bathroom, as large as the living room, was attached to the back of the house with no possibility of any heat reaching there from the old coal heating stove at the front of the house. Taking a bath was a shivering experience, especially in the winter. On very cold nights we had to run the bathtub full of boiling water and let this stand all night to keep the pipes in that room from freezing and bursting.

Around the house there was plenty of yard—no grass, but plenty of space. There was dirt to dig and sand to play in, but Jimmy always found the unusual thing. This time it was the gas tank of the car. To protect the car from the storms which usually came from the north, I parked it on the south side of the house, near the back porch by the big pile of sand and rocks where Jimmy played.

One Saturday we hustled through our work, put on our "steppin' harness" as the cowboys called dress-up clothes, and started for Bozeman. We got as far as the Madison Bridge when the car stopped. The children were too little to help me push the car, and I could not push it alone and steer—but I tried. I was unsuccessfully straining at this when the highway patrolman stopped behind me.

"What in the world is this?" he said very sharply. "Oh, it's you, Mrs. Doig. Having trouble?" His daughter was in my freshman English class.

I didn't know whether to be funny or respectful. It might cost me something if I smarted off too much.

"I don't know what's the matter, but it stopped—the car, I mean," I said.

"Out of gas?" He smiled patronizingly at a woman's foibles.

I started to snap back a retort but bit my lip and said, "I'm sure I have gas."

Of course he did not believe me and stepped out of his car to look in at the dashboard panel. He turned on the key, watched the needle point to half full, turned off the key.

"Got to get you off this bridge." He nudged the patrol car against the bumper of my car and began to push us ahead and off the bridge. He helped us turn the car around and then pushed it back to Three Forks and in front of a garage. The mechanic there started with the gas pump.

"Sand in here," he called out, his head under the hood. He removed the pump and the acetylene bulb. After rinsing out the sand he followed the gas line. More sand.

"Have to take off the tank and drain and clean it. You'd better go on home and come back tomorrow."

The children and I walked up the street. I looked from one to the other.

"Anyone know anything about this sand in the gas tank?"

Beverly was the first to answer. Very soberly and slowly she shook her head. "Why, no, Mother."

Margie and Marilyn just shook their heads, always simultaneously. Joan shook hers until her curls bounced. Jimmy did not look up. He walked ahead, kicking at the dust with the toes of his shoes.

"Jimmy, did you put sand in the gas tank?"

"Guess I did."

"Why did you do such a thing?"

"Playin' like it vas das [gas] and I vas doin' to make it do [go]." Jimmy was the slowest one to learn to speak well.

I groaned, and we walked on. "How much sand, Jimmy?"
"Oh, lots and lots. Doin' to take a long twip."

I did not punish him. He was so serious. I talked to him about what he had done and about how much trouble it would cause all of us. But for weeks that car was the "bane of my existence." I never went more than a few miles without having to get out and clean sand from the gas pump or the gas line. For months I was afraid to drive anywhere far from home at night. The car could not be trusted. It would stop at the most inconvenient times and places.

Then one Friday after school we decided to accept the Springers' invitation to have dinner at their home, a ranch up on the Toston flats about ten miles north of us. The children were delighted with the idea. There would be kittens and dogs and other animals, and youngsters about their ages. The car purred along all the way, not a cough or a choke or a sputter.

On the way home, at the first gate, when I started to drive through the gateway, the car died as I stepped on the accelerator. It was dark and I had not even a flashlight. Leaving the sleepy children, I walked the half mile back to the ranch house to borrow a lantern. Mr. Springer returned to the car with me, the lantern swinging between us, making a little spot of light around us. Together we cleaned out the acetylene bulb, the gas pump, part of the gas line, and worked until the car started and I was again on my way toward Three Forks.

For almost a year I didn't trust that car. By the time all the sand was out of the tank and the line, I had learned much about the "innards" of an automobile.

CHAPTER TWENTY-SEVEN

Beverly should have been a boy. The doctor said all the time before she was born that she was going to be. The fetal heart tones were very strong and slow. In the delivery room her father and I had talked about names for a boy. When she was born, I heard her strong cry as the doctor slapped her to make sure she was breathing. I asked, "What is it, Doctor?"

"Oh, it's a boy. No, wait a minute! By gosh, it's a girl." The nurses laughed with him.

We took her home to the ranch, and the cowboys adored her. Soon they were tossing her up in the air, playing with her roughly. I always said that Beverly would never know when she was being punished because she was accoustomed to being spanked so much in fun. The cowboys taught her to walk. I was afraid they would teach her to talk—cowboy talk!

She enjoyed dogs, chickens, horses . . . never learned the meaning of fear. By the time she was a year old, she was out of doors most of the time. Often I would find her in the chicken yard sitting down with a pan of wheat and feeding the hens from her hands. She would share her cookie or sandwich with Tuffy, the big cow dog on the ranch. If I did not watch her she would eat hotcakes from his pan by the back door.

Beverly would wander about the ranch house, down to the corrals, the barns, by herself. When I did not find her in the house, I would step to the door and call out, "Beverly." From various places she would call back, "Begerly," her name for herself.

Although we were very careful about not talking baby talk to her, she developed her own names for many articles. Her stockings were her "ti-ta's"; her shoes, "ow's"; her dress was a "pretty"; her panties were "oh, my."

She was on a saddle horse with her daddy long before she could walk, sitting in front, hanging on to the horn. At night when he took off his cowboy boots she would manage to get her feet into them and try to walk. She would say, "Mama, if I faw down in dese, I be in a 'dicament!"

Whenever Jim was near the ranch house, she was his shadow. If he went to the pump to get a bucket of water, she had her little pail and filled it too. Often when he went to town to the stock sales ring to watch the cattle being sold, she would go along, sitting between his knees on the backless board seats until she fell asleep. Then he would hold her in his arms until the sale was over.

When he died she was almost four. She lost her best friend, her comrade, her adored parent. I was so busy with the two sets of twins that Beverly had to do many things for herself. She missed her daddy poignantly—especially about dusk. She would get her little red chair and go to the low window in the kitchen and sit looking out.

"Mommy, when will my daddy come home?" she would ask. I would explain carefully. She wouldn't cry—just sit there looking. But the next night it would be the same thing. Over and over again this was repeated.

As she grew older, she thought things out for herself. She had to be independent. She was never "little girlish" like her three sisters.

One evening, when she was six years old, I came home from school, walked around the house to where the children were playing in the backyard, and started to push Jimmy in the swing. All at once I noticed Joyce, Beverly's school chum. All around one eye the flesh was black and swollen.

"Joyce," I said laughingly, "where did you get that black eye?"

"Beverly gived it to me," she said unconcernedly.

"What!" I yipped. That had wiped the grin off my face. "How?"

"Oh, Beverly hit me." And she went on with the mud pie she was making.

"Beverly, did you hit Joyce?"

"Yes, I did."

"But why?"

"'Cause she punched me hard in the tummy and it hurt so I hit her." Just as matter-of-fact as that!

I was horrified. I could just see Joyce's mother coming irately to the house when she saw her daughter's eye. What should I do? I talked and talked to the girls. They weren't interested. They were perfectly good friends now that the difference between them had been settled. I fussed over the altercation, apologized to the mother, but did not manage to touch the unruffled disposition of the little girls. Like two boys they had settled their quarrel, and that was that!

CHAPTER TWENTY-EIGHT

"Mrs. Doig, will you come to the telephone in the office, please?" The student pulled her head back out of my classroom door and closed it.

I laid the literature book on my desk.

"You can finish reading the story," I said over my shoulder to the class and hurried out of the room.

A phone call—nobody ever called me. It frightened me, because I had two brothers in the Armed Forces. I ran down the stairs and up the hall to the office. The office girl nodded toward the waiting telephone receiver and smiled at my anxious look.

"Hello, hello!" I shouted into the mouthpiece.

The voice that answered was a familiar one.

"Hi, Elsie. Know who this is?"

"You tell me who it is," I said. It was a long-distance call; I could tell by the sound of the wires.

"This is Fred Stone. You haven't forgotten me, have you? How are you?"

"Of course I haven't. I'm okay. But where are you, Fred?"

"Right here at Crowalls' ranch. Just got in from the Japanese war area by way of San Francisco. My leave is only for ten days. Say, how about coming out Saturday and playing for my—for our wedding? Huh? Can do?"

"Fred, you're not old enough. Don't tell me you've talked Shirley into marrying you!"

Fred's laugh was real, even over the poor telephone connections.

"Of course I'll play for your wedding. Where will it be? When? Is it formal?"

"Now, one at a time. At Dry Creek Church, Saturday, two o'clock in the afternoon. Nope, not formal. Say, and will you sing too?"

"Oh, now, Fred, I *like* those people. I can't pull that on them." He knew I would.

"Can you get out here? That old heap of junk of yours still running?"

"No comments on my car. Of course it runs. I'll be there early so we can practice."

"See you then," he said, and the connection was ended.

"Oh, no—I forgot to ask him to get an accompanist for me," I mumbled as I thanked the office girl and started back to my classroom.

Friday evening I went home from school walking on winged feet. A whole day visiting with ranch friends—what fun! But the housekeeper met me at the door, and her face wore a worried expression.

"Margie's sick. I suppose it's flu. She's feverish, and her throat is bad."

Into the bedroom I hurried, shedding my coat and scarf as I went, and laid my cold hand on her flushed face. The contrast startled me. I stooped to kiss her and pushed her hair from her forehead. Her troubled eyes followed every motion. The other children clustered around.

"Beverly, bring me the thermometer from the medicine cabinet," I called as I pulled off my overshoes.

Obediently, Margie opened her lips to let the fever thermometer in. As I waited for it to register, I listened to the other children's experiences of the day. I sat on the edge of the bed, lifted Joan to my lap, and set Jimmy beside me.

Taking the thermometer from Margie's mouth, I held it above me to try to read it. Drat those things! I never could read a thermometer without turning it around several times. The mercury showed 103 degrees. Not dangerous for a child, I knew, but not good. I put Joan down and went into the kitchen.

"Do you suppose if I talked to the doctor here in Three Forks he could tell me what to do?" I asked my house-keeper as I shook the thermometer to lower the mercury.

"Good idea," she said, and she stooped to look into the oven where a roast was cooking.

"Be back in a minute," I called to the children and ran out the door and over to the house of a neighbor to use her telephone.

The doctor's calm voice reassured me. "Give her half an aspirin. Bathe her in lukewarm water. Sounds like flu. I'll be around to see her early in the morning."

By bedtime Margie's temperature was down to 100 de-grees, and I continued my preparations for going to Fred's wedding. My housekeeper offered to stay Saturday until I got home again.

"You'll be okay tomorrow," I promised, as I kissed Margie and Marilyn good-night, turned out their light, and went to tuck in the other children. Several times during the evening I went to the room to check her temperature by laying a hand on her forehead. She was restless, but a drink of water and a bit of petting quieted her.

Early in the morning, I laid out my clothes and ran boiling water in the bathtub to warm the cold room. When I heard Margie's hoarse voice, I hurried to her bed. The daylight was just graying, so I turned on a light. I must have gasped, for Marilyn said, "Mother, what's the matter?"

"Look at Margie. She's speckled like a turkey egg.

Marilyn, can you bring the mirror so we can show her?"

Tiny red spots covered her face and neck. We pulled back the covers—yes, her legs and body were broken out too.

"What on earth do you have, Margie dear?" I asked.

"Can't be chicken pox, Mother. We had that last year," Beverly observed as she directed Marilyn's hand so that the mirror would give Margie a view of herself.

"I better get the doctor over here right away," I said, "or I'll never make it to that wedding."

The doctor came, examined, looked again, took her temperature—and stood with his hand on his chin. Motioning me out into the kitchen he said in a low voice, "Looks like scarlet fever. But I don't know of any cases of it here in Three Forks. I'll have to place you all under quarantine."

"Oh, no," I said, "I'm to play for a wedding today. Oh, doctor, are you sure it is scarlet fever? Her temperature is almost normal now."

"Well, let's see. Have you given her anything—any medicine?"

"Only the aspirin you prescribed. She's never had aspirin before. Could it have been that?"

"Slim chance. A few people are allergic to aspirin—but very few. Now, I'll tell you what. You hang your clothes out the bathroom window. It's cold as the dickens outside. Take a fresh bath, put on these freshly aired clothes— everything you wear, mind you—none of your false modesty, young woman! If you climb out the window after you're dressed and don't come back into the house I guess I'll let you go to that wedding."

He stepped back into the bedroom and called cheerily, "You be a good girl and stay in bed all day. Breakfast in bed. Won't that be fun? See you tomorrow, Mrs. Doig." And he was gone.

I looked ruefully at my housekeeper and then hurried to hang my clothes outside. I loosened the screen on the bathroom window. It was just nailed onto the window casing. One by one I pulled out the tacks and dropped them into my coat pocket, blowing on my numb fingers. It really was cold! With the screen off, I pushed up the window a ways and hooked the clothes hangers—covered with my one suit and blouse and underthings—over the ledge.

After many last-minute preparations and explanations to the children, I closed the bathroom door to begin my bath. The clothes were icy cold when I pulled them in and put them on. Luckily there was a chair in the bathroom. The window was small, and about four feet from the back porch floor. I'm not noted for my agility, but I managed to get through the window and onto the ground with no mishaps.

Hurrying to the car, which I had started before and left running, I drove rapidly away.

The wedding was a success—oh, not in a social way. Its informalities would have been frowned upon by the world of society. But this was the first wedding ever to be performed in the little Dry Creek Church. It established a precedent for church weddings in that community. After the ceremony the bride and groom sat in the living room of the old ranch house of the Crowalls and visited with their friends as they ate sandwiches, cake, and all sorts of food.

Everyone asked Fred questions. He had finished fifty bombing missions on the plane in which he was the pilot. He did not have to return to combat duty abroad. Shirley realized how fortunate she was to have him home, unharmed. Her eyes were like stars when she looked at him as he told of those dangerous trips in the bomber—Fred, whom we thought of as just a run-of-the-mill cowboy was now a pilot in the Air Force! The exigencies of fate often make heroes of ordinary boys. The war seemed closer than ever that day.

It was dark when I drove up beside the little brown house in Three Forks. Lights shone from every window. The forty miles of driving had given me time to ponder Margie's illness. Would we be quarantined for scarlet fever? Now how could I manage this dilemma? I must not be absent from school.

The back door of the house flew open as the car's engine stopped, and four children ran out onto the back porch and stood calling to me.

"Margie's better, Mother," I heard above the other bits of information called to me, "and her spots are almost gone."

"It was just the aspirin," my housekeeper said to me.

Tension slipped from my nerves like water running down a slight incline. Not scarlet fever, then! "Oh, thank you, Lord," I said, as I opened the petcock on the radiator to let out the water, and then put the hood back down. "Again you've helped me out in a tight pinch, Lord, and I'm thankful." And I hurried into the house to my waiting children.

CHAPTER TWENTY-NINE

It was March of 1944. The war was at its highest pitch. In school we bought savings stamps and war bonds. Seniors in my English classes were restless and inattentive. The boys knew that if they enlisted they would be granted a diploma, whether they finished the school year or not. The girls were emotionally upset over the boys' being drafted and going away.

I had one brother in pilot training school; another had just won his navigator wings. A week before Easter a letter came from the navigator, Kenneth. He was now in Boise, Idaho. He and his crew were getting acquainted with each other and their brand-new B-24 which they would fly to a combat area soon. For a few weeks he would be studying celestial navigation—"Shooting the stars," he called it.

"Why don't you come out for a weekend and visit me?" he wrote. "I can pay for your trip. Officer's pay seems like a lot of money to me. I have nothing special to spend it on."

I answered him immediately. "I have four days with no school next weekend—Easter vacation. How about my leaving here Thursday night?"

His answering telegram came the day after that. "Have hotel room reserved for you. Will meet your bus."

My housekeeper promised to stay with the children over the weekend; I would pay her extra for it. The children looked somewhat bleak when I told them of my contemplated trip. They went with me to the drugstore that served as bus depot to buy a ticket. We discovered that the bus I would return on would reach Three Forks Sunday morning at nine o'clock, so I would be home in time to go to the

Easter service with the children. That brightened the gloom considerably. As we walked home we talked about the new Easter dresses I had just finished making for them—blue for Margie and Marilyn, with pink flowers appliqued on the skirts and collars, and pink for Joan and Beverly with blue applique.

"How 'bout me? How 'bout me?" Jimmy wanted to be in on this too.

"You have new blue corduroy pants; don't you remember? And I made a white shirt for you."

"But the Easter bunny, Mother," Beverly said. She no longer believed in one, but we had agreed—she and I—to let the twins continue to think there was an Easter bunny . . . at least for a while.

"That's been taken care of," I assured her and winked carefully, over the twins' heads.

Everyone had some part in packing the suitcase. Even Jimmy helped, bringing shoe after shoe until he got the right ones. They all sat up to wait until bus time but were too sleepy to walk with me to the drugstore.

The bus was crowded with passengers, many service men and women besides the regular number of travelers. I edged my way to the back and squeezed into the last seat, across the end, along with four other adults, two GI's and two girls in WAC uniforms. One of the girls had a figure that bulged in all the wrong places. She had a strident, almost masculine laugh. She squeezed against the GI beside her, but he seemed not too interested. At every stop of the bus, the GI's got off, coming back each time with voices louder and noisier. By midnight they were quite drunk. The one WAC found the GI beside her more responsive to her advances. His head lolled on her shoulder. Now and again she kissed him. By morning they were wrapped in each other's arms, his head on her capacious breasts.

The excitement and the discomfort drove all idea of sleep from my mind. When we stopped at Idaho Falls to change buses, we had to wait almost an hour. Several slot machines stood along one wall of the waiting room. With fascination I watched people plugging nickels into the maws of these iron robbers. Back in a corner a ragged boy about seven years old fed one nickel after another into a machine. At last, having no more money, he stood a moment frowning, then began to hit the machine with both fists. A stream of coins fell to the floor. Quickly he grabbed them and stuffed his pockets. Just then the door opened. Someone came in and over to the corner where the boy stood and shoved him out of the way, growling, "Listen, sonny, no one can win playing slot machines. Now get out of here."

The boy said not a word, but with an enigmatic smile on his face he slipped out of the door and hurried away.

I heard my bus called and took my place in the waiting line. A few more hours of riding and I was in Boise. As the bus drove into the station, I scanned the waiting crowd for my brother. At first I did not recognize him. I had never seen him in uniform. He took my suitcase and we went to the hotel, a few blocks away, left my luggage, then took a bus out to the air base to eat lunch. He took me to a table where the men of his crew ate together. One by one each man assumed for me the personality Kenneth had described in his letters. The comradery which stayed with them in all of their bombing trips over Europe was already developing. The other fellows were kidding my brother and calling him "parson." He had played for a wedding of one of the crew the week before, right there on the base.

Proudly Kenneth took me to the officers' club to wait until he had finished his classes. I felt a bit of reflected glory as I walked beside him and watched the men salute him—my little brother whom I had taken care of when he was a baby. As he left me, I turned to the rows of magazine racks. What luxury to have the choice of so much free reading, and the time to do it! I sank into a soft chair and forgot the world about me.

Later we went to a restaurant for dinner. Kenneth ordered steaks for us. "The waiters cater to the officers," he said with his old grin.

Afterward we decided on a movie. It was one of those melodramatic stories. We laughed hilariously at the tear-jerking scenes. Together we ridiculed the contrived plots, the exaggerated emotions, the unmotivated actions of the characters.

"You know, Kenneth," I said as I wiped my eyes, "I haven't laughed like this since before Jim died. Somehow it cleans the cobwebs out of my soul."

Back in my hotel, I dawdled over a warm bath, creamed my face luxuriously, and read a magazine until I fell asleep—secure in the knowledge that I could sleep until late and no child would call to wake me.

"It's raining," Kenneth called from the hall next morning when I opened the door to his knock.

"Who's afraid of rain?" I asked.

He took me to the air base and left me at the club after we had eaten a leisurely breakfast. I wandered through the rooms, sat in the comfortable chairs, found some stationery to write letters. When Kenneth picked me up at noon we went to the dining room, where we again ate with his crew. It was fun to be the only woman in the large dining room. For the first time in four years I felt as if

I were a woman—not just a mother of five, not just the English teacher, but a woman!

"Why don't you go with me to the place where I study celestial navigation and then find your way back to the officers' club?" Kenneth suggested. "It is not very far to walk." He took me into a round, silo-like building and showed me his sextant, the seats that could be whirled, then told me somewhat of his training. He explained the importance of having a watch that kept absolutely perfect time.

"If it is off even a fraction of a second," he said, "I won't know where our plane is," and he pulled back his cuff to show a beautiful Elgin wristwatch. "As navigator, I have to tell the pilot how to guide the plane back to the air base when we break squadron formation after the bombs have been dropped on a target."

"And if you should set the plane down on the spire of a French cathedral, then what?"

"I worry about that," he said seriously. "First few weeks up in the plane I was so scared that I lost my cookies every trip, but I'm okay now. Just nerves, the doctor said."

I saw the other navigators coming in. "Shall I go now?"

He nodded. "Meet you at two o'clock."

Leisurely I walked toward the officers' club. Nothing to hurry about! No one needing to be cared for! My time my own! I hugged this thought to myself. I went into the cafeteria and ordered an ice-cream sundae. When it came, I must have gasped for the waitress said quickly, "Isn't this right?"

"Oh, yes," I said quickly. But I had never seen such a helping of ice cream before. It wasn't just a dish full—it was a bowl! There was mound after mound of various kinds of ice cream, each with a different topping. My eyes bulged as I picked up the spoon. I never did get all that ice cream stowed away, but I ate slow bites of it for a long time, enjoying the idea of having more than I could eat—and all this for fifteen cents.

When Kenneth arrived we took a bus to town.

"What would you like to do?" he asked. A light rain was falling. The streetlights had been turned on, making spots of misty radiance along the street.

"Let's go to a music store," I suggested. I had taught him all the music he had had until he began to take piano lessons in college.

We browsed through pieces of music, trying out first one and then another. Sometimes he would play; sometimes I would.

"Is there any particular piece you would like—or a book of pieces? I want to buy you something," he said.

"A book of preludes for church service would make me happy."

He searched for one like his own favorite book, but did not find it. He chose another—one that included Chopin and other "powder-puff" music as he called it. Putting the purchase under his arm beneath his raincoat, he led the way out into the rain again. At a bookstore we stopped. Moving slowly up and down the rows of books, we discussed the merits of various writers, arguing about this and that favorite author.

"Seems odd for you to be a navigator when your majors in college were in language and music," I mused.

"Did I ever tell you what happened when I first entered the Air Corps?" asked Kenneth, turning away from my observation.

I shook my head.

"Well, the test was a stinker. I was scared of the math and science questions so I skipped the English section and started on the math first. I never did remember to go back to the English questions. I was sent to Eau Claire, Wisconsin, to a college to brush up on math and English. After about a week the English instructor called me up after class and said, 'What the heck are you doing in my English classes? I looked up your record and found your college English credits—all A's. Besides your essays are better than those of my seniors.' Then I remembered the forgotten English section of that test!"

"Did you stay in that class?"

"No, but I really grubbed in those math classes. You know how I hate math."

He picked up a book and leafed through it. "Like Cronin?" he asked.

"I haven't read much of his writing."

"I think you'll like this, I did. It's light, romantic, easy, and relaxing." He walked over to the cash register. With the packages under his raincoat, we wandered on from store to store.

"Hey, it's five thirty; we'd better head for the hotel and the bus depot." As we walked we became serious.

"Kenneth, where do you go from here?"

"We take our own plane across," he said thoughtfully, "flying in a squadron. Might be North Africa; could be Italy; may be the South Pacific."

"I know that in your letters you can't tell us where you are going, but you can describe the things you see so we'll have some idea of where you are."

"Yes, I'll manage to let you know."

We walked on.

"Kenneth, are you afraid of death?" I asked.

"I don't know," he said slowly. "I suppose I am. Everyone is."

"Don't be afraid. When Jim died I looked death squarely in the face and found myself wanting to die. It was much harder to live. Death is not an unhappy experience. It is those who remain here who have the real struggle. Life is not easy. How many times I've resented my children because they held me here on earth—made me live to take care of them."

Neither of us spoke for a block or more.

"There's your bus, I'll bet," he said suddenly. "Says Butte, Montana, on the front. Shall we run for it?" My suitcase bumping against his legs, we ran laughingly into the depot and out to the waiting bus. The passengers were loaded on, but the bus did not take off. The driver started the engine several times, but still we did not move. Kenneth came to my window and stood under it. We began to talk. We laughed and joked. For thirty minutes the bus stood there, but Kenneth and I did not notice the time. We were back in our childhood on the homestead in eastern Montana. One by one we recalled humorous experiences.

"Remember the time Jerome bought that sack of candy for his girl and you and Ralph drilled holes in the bottom of each piece and packed in that terrible red pepper?" he reminisced.

"Do I? And then Jerome caught me and forced one of the chocolates into my mouth and made me bite down on it. Wow, my mouth burned for a day!"

The other passengers on the bus were listening and enjoying our chatter too.

"Yeah, and the time Ammon chopped down on my head instead of the wild turnip hole where he was digging?"

The past seemed so much more real, more secure than the present. Unconsciously we had turned to it. We gained confidence to face the future as we recalled humorous, even dangerous, situations that we had experienced. Standing there in the light rain, with head tipped back, laughing carelessly, he seemed like my little brother again. The lieutenant bars on his shoulder were unreal. The navigator's wings were merely a pin. Again I felt the surge of older-sister protectiveness. Why should this boy leave his home, his country, to fight in a war? He was such a fun-loving, peace-loving boy—the baby of the family. He didn't hate people or things; he never had. What would war and combat do to him?

The driver started the motor again, and slowly the bus began to move.

"*Auf wiedersehen,*" I called.

"*Leben sie wohl,*" he answered and smiled and waved.

I leaned back against the seat and held tightly to my emotions until I could think calmly.

*   *   *   *   *

Bright sunshine flooded the valley and glanced from the snow-topped mountain peaks as the bus pulled to a stop by the station in Three Forks the next morning. Carrying my suitcase, I walked the few blocks to our house. As I neared it, I saw the back door flung open and five figures raced down the walk toward me. Dropping my suitcase and stooping to their level, I gathered them into my arms.

"Was it fun, Mother?"

"Did you see Uncle Kenneth?"

"The Easter rabbit comed."

Listening to their eager chatter, I knew how very precious these children were to me. It had been good to get away, but it was also good to be back. The war and its problems slipped away from me for the present. Here was my work to do.

CHAPTER THIRTY

In the spring we moved into a big comfortable house at the end of the street, across from the principal's home. There was a good-sized front porch, a place for a tricycle and a bike. The rooms were large and high-ceilinged. In the living and dining rooms were wide panels of rich, polished oak. Shining oak beams above the fireplace in one corner reflected the light of the flames when we had a fire. In the entry hall a curving stairway ascended to the second floor, an oak window and seat halfway up.

In the dining room I had my sewing machine where I sat many hours making the children's clothes for the year, often listening through the open windows to the chatter of the children or watching them at play in the tree-shaded yard. Here I brought my ironing board, and on the big table I corrected essays and wrote out exams during the school year.

In the basement we had a good furnace which gave even heat to all of the house. Crooked stairs that wound around and around led us down there. A room with thick walls, no windows, and a heavy door had shelves and bins for the jars of canned vegetables and fruit, for the potatoes and carrots and cabbages.

I had a garden in a vacant lot a few blocks away. The children helped me put the long hose into the little wagon and take it there at least once a week. Setting a large sprinkler, I would walk back and forth every hour to change the water to a different spot.

It was a good place to live. We were warm in the winter and cool in the summer. People were very friendly in this little town. I wanted to do something in return. So I played the piano for the services in the local federated church and taught the class for high school students.

Marilyn and Margie started to school that fall. Beverly was in the third grade. Mornings were a busy time as I braided the hair on the top of the twins' heads and brushed the sides. Beverly's French braids took longer to do. Often we all walked to school together, but usually I went a while before they did. Neighbors, watching the three girls passing by on their way to and from school, commented on the bright dresses which they wore. Anna helped me make them colorful with gay little animals and flowers appliqued on skirts in interesting designs.

When Marilyn and Margie started to school in the fall, Jim and Joan were lonely at first, missing the accustomed companionship. Every evening they waited at the edge of our lawn, eager to hear each event of the day at school.

In November, Anna and her husband went to Arizona, where he worked in a munitions plant for the winter. They brought the old cow dog, Bo, that had been on our ranch, to stay with us. Quickly he adopted the children . . . spent every minute with them when they were out of doors. School mornings he would walk sedately between them, down the street to the schoolhouse. As they went up the steps, he would stand waiting on the sidewalk until the door closed behind them. Turning he would trot back to the house to lie near Jim and Joan as they played.

At the exact time each afternoon when school would be out for first graders, he appeared near the schoolhouse door, waiting patiently while students came down the steps, chattering like squirrels. The twins would stop in their conversation with the other children to say, "Hello, Bo," and put a hand on his head. He would stand quietly until they began to move down the street, one twin on each side of him.

It was very cold that winter. We had difficulty getting Bo to sleep in the basement at night. The first few times I had to carry him there—a heavy load. In the morning he whined gently from the top step of the basement stairs, waiting to get let out of doors.

In Montana in the mountainous country, winters are long. Snow often lies on the ground from November to April, even in the valleys. But the big furnace kept us warm even when the temperature outside dropped to forty degrees below zero. The house was well built, sturdy, never a squeak of timbers when strong winds would swoop down the valley.

One night, after a particularly severe cold season, when the children were in bed and asleep, I went to the basement as usual to fill and adjust the furnace for the night. As I opened the coal room door, I saw water pouring out across the floor of the basement. In a panic I began to look up at water pipes, following them until I found a cutout valve on a pipe that led to the coal room. Standing on an old stool, I turned the wheel to shut off the water. As I worked, I remembered an outside faucet near the window that opened into the coal room. By this time the water was over an inch deep around the furnace and on the cement floor nearby. Jumping from dry spot to spot I ran back upstairs to get overshoes and flashlight, and again came down the crooked, narrow stairway and into the dark coal room. Flashing my light on the outside wall, I quickly located the culprit, a partly open window near the water pipe that had caused that pipe to freeze and burst. Scrambling up onto the coal, I climbed and slid until I finally reached the window, closed it securely, wondering whether the children had opened it or the coal man had not closed it securely the last time he had brought coal. It did not matter now, except that I had an onerous job to do.

Water was rapidly covering most of that part of the basement floor. There was no floor drain. Taking a big tub from the wall in the washroom, I picked up a coal shovel and began to scoop up the water and lift it into the tub. When the tub was filled I carried it up the winding stairs and emptied it into the kitchen sink. This was backbreaking, so I found a five-gallon bucket and filled it. Scoop and carry, scoop and carry—until the water was not running so freely.

Water was still seeping from the coal room. I found an extension cord with a socket and a bulb, rigged it to a nail in a rafter in the ceiling of the coal room, and looked around. There was much water under part of the coal. Taking the shovel, I began to move the water-soaked coal from the one side of the room to the dry places. I moved at least a ton of coal before I stopped to scoop water from the floor into my bucket again. When I could get less than a cup of water each time, I brought the broom and swept the water into pools and then scooped it up. My arms ached and my back felt permanently bent, but I knew this must be done.

Later I brought the mop, sopping up the water and wringing it out into the pail. There were still a few wet places when I stopped. I filled the furnace with some of the dry coal, went up the stairs to take a bath and go to bed. It was very late.

The next day I called a plumber to repair the broken pipe.

The Greeks wrote that we learn by what we suffer. Well, I learned to watch that window in the coal room.

CHAPTER THIRTY-ONE

Absorbed though I was in my children, I was also very much interested in my students at school. Each new class of young people brought a heterogeneous group with individual problems and interests. Some students were enjoyable from the beginning. Some I had to learn to love.

The first day of school was really just teachers' meetings and preparation. After most of the faculty had gone home, I sat at my desk looking through my pile of registration cards for senior English classes. Suddenly I groaned, "Oh, no! Not again!"

"Talking to yourself, Mrs. Doig?" The assistant principal put his head around the open door and grinned. "You know what that's a sign of."

"Yes, and you'd go crazy yourself if you had to put up with that boy another year."

"Let's see—could I venture a guess? You are talking about Jorrie Roberts?" Mr. Watson came into the room and telescoped his tall, lanky body into a student's desk directly before me.

"Yes, I am." I scowled and shook my head. "I had him last year in junior English class. Two other teachers had kicked him out of their classes, and you gave him to me. Well, I put up with him and his nonsense for almost a year and I just . . . I just . . ."

"I know, I know. But Mrs. Doig, you're the only one who will take him. You seem to understand boys, especially troublesome ones. Jorrie wanted to take this English class— signed up for it himself when he knew it wasn't required.

When I asked him why, he muttered, 'She's the only teacher who likes me, I reckon.' "

"Just because I'm a pushover," I said sourly.

"We don't want to expel him. That would put him on the streets and in the beer joints. Even if we can't teach him anything out of a book, let's try to keep him in school." He jiggled his wristwatch a moment. "Have you looked at the record of his family?"

"Yes, I have." Some of my resentment was slipping away. "Nothing where the name of the father should be. Someone told me this summer that Jorrie's mother refuses to support him, doesn't want him around. He has a room somewhere and works at odd jobs during the school year."

Unfolding his long legs, Mr. Watson stood up. "You know why I am trying to keep him here one more year then. I can count on you, I'm sure. If anyone can get next to him, you can."

"Don't count on it—but I'll try." I picked up the registration cards and began to look through them again. The assistant principal went on down the hall.

School began next day with its usual clatter and confusion. Freshmen lost their way, were sent to the wrong rooms by grinning seniors and juniors. Classes ground on to the last period of the day.

Before the last class, I steeled myself as for an attack. Here would be several of the most recalcitrant students. It would be murder to allow them to go to the study hall this hour. Pity the study hall teacher! And here, of course, in this hour I would have Jorrie. I could hear his raucous laugh as he neared my door.

"Come on in, kids, and suffer awhile," I heard him say as he led the way into the room. My smile felt fixed, as if it had been painted on my face. As the class crowded into the back seats of the room, I glanced over the students and catalogued each one in my mind. Two of Jorrie's satellites were there too! That meant real trouble. There must be an easier way to earn a living than teaching, I thought. Well, I would try to find some other kind of work next year.

The second week of school it was my turn to help chaperon the school youth-center activity. Mr. Adams from social science came to help me. He sat at the downstairs door and admitted the students, checking their cards. I watched the upstairs rooms. As the hours dragged on, the voices seemed noisier, especially those of several boys. One boy almost fell against me as he passed. His breath reeked with the smell of liquor.

"That's queer," I said to myself. "They're not allowed to go out of the building and come in again." I began to watch one gang—Jorrie's—more closely. They kept going downstairs and coming up again later, each time noisier and more insolent. But students always milled around so much— I couldn't judge by that.

Midnight came, and my whole body sagged with weariness as I watched the last stragglers leave. I went down the stairs to the first floor and on down the hall. Suddenly I stopped. There were voices coming from the boys' washroom.

Turning, I called up the stairs, "Mr. Adams, you up there?"

"Be with you in a minute." His voice echoed in the empty corridors.

I stood still in the hall and listened. The sound of boys' talking died away, but no one had come out of the door I was watching. The roar of a motor with twin pipes sounded distinctly from behind the school building.

Mr. Adams' feet appeared at the top of the stairs, then his knees and finally his head as he came sedately down the steps, pushing his paunchy middle ahead of him.

"Everyone gone, Mrs. Doig? Doesn't the quiet seem good?"

"No, not all gone; there are boys in there yet." I nodded my head toward the boys' room.

Mr. Adams opened the door and stuck his head into the room. "Empty," he called out, then went on, "Hey, what's this?"

The janitor, coming around the corner of the hall just then, answered him. "I think I can tell you what you want to know. Jorrie Roberts' car was parked just back of this room in the parking lot and . . ."

"Hey, what are all those bottles and cans doing in here? Yeah, and the windows are both open. Now what in the world . . ."

"I think Jorrie furnished the liquor for tonight—or his gang did—and it came in by way of the windows of this room. I shoulda' caught on sooner. If that kid don't beat all!" The janitor was muttering under his breath.

I just stood there shaking my head. Jorrie—those boys going up and down the stairs—why hadn't I guessed it? Yes, I could have him expelled. But what would I gain? I'll talk to him alone, I thought. And I went wearily on down the hall and let myself out the front door, so intense in my thinking that I had walked two blocks past my parked car before I realized it.

The talk with Jorrie next day produced no effects. There seemed to be no way to appeal to him. But I didn't like to accept defeat, and I tried every trick in the bag. Over the years I had built up some knowledge of boys. I had scolded them, censured them, forgiven them, tried to under-

179

stand them. But nothing I tried brought any good results from this boy.

One cold February afternoon Jorrie wasn't in class. I was concerned because he seldom missed school—wouldn't miss the chance to torture me, I was sure. The class was so quiet, so peaceful, it was portentous.

"Where's Jorrie?" I asked one of his gang as the students filed out with the last bell.

"Dunno, unless he's sick."

"Would one of you boys look him up tonight?"

"Guess we could. Usually go to his room to play po—, I mean to his hangout every night."

I thought no more about it until the next afternoon when Jorrie's desk was empty again.

"Did you boys see Jorrie last night?" I asked after class.

"Yeah, he's sick, awful sick. We wanted to call a doc, but he cussed at us and said docs didn't know nothin'."

"Perhaps you should call his mother."

The boys looked at each other and shook their heads. "Naw, she don't care about him, won't do nothin' for him."

"Well, if he isn't better tonight, you fellows call Doctor Brunen. He's the county doctor and will come without pay. Will you do that?"

They nodded briefly and hurried away. The next morning one of the gang slipped into my room before school.

"Jorrie's in the hospital. Double pneumonia, doctor said. Bawled us out for not callin' him sooner. That's gratitude for you," he said quickly and left.

All day long I thought of Jorrie. Being class sponsor, I felt more responsible for the seniors. Often we sent cards or gifts to members who were very ill. To each class of seniors I said, "Say, Jorrie Roberts is in the hospital with pneumonia. Can some of you drop in to see him or send him a card?"

The next day I managed to find time to go to the hospital after school. Jorrie's room had a big placard on it: "No Visitors." But as the days went on his condition gradually improved. The senior class sent flowers. Then he developed a severe reaction to the drugs that had been given him. He was very sick. Blisters formed all over the inside of his mouth and down his throat.

The students had formed the habit of dropping in to visit him in the evening whenever he was allowed visitors. He was deluged with cards. As he began to convalesce, his room in the hospital became a meeting place for the high school students.

"Gotta go down and pep up Jorrie," they would say. Or, "Hey, been to see Jorrie lately? He can tell the funniest stories!" Students who had never been friendly toward him, who had treated him as a stray mongrel, found time to visit him in the hospital.

I found a foolish toy, a Pluto dog that moved with strings, and a book about hot rods to take with me when I finally did go to the hospital. I was amazed at Jorrie's sunken cheeks and colorless skin, but I liked what I could detect of the change in him. He had relaxed under all the attention. His hangdog expression which had always been covered by a shell of bravado had disappeared. He was still so weak he couldn't sit up, but he joked and laughed with the students as if he were one of their group.

Jorrie was out of school for six weeks. It was a long up-hill grind—his return to health. His undernourished body was hard put to it to survive at all. One evening in March a sound at the classroom door caused me to lift my tired eyes from the essays I was correcting and turn them in the direction of the door. There stood Jorrie, as cocky as ever.

For a second or two the classroom atmosphere put the chip on his shoulder, then he shrugged and walked slowly across the room and leaned against the windowsill. His faded Levi's hung loosely on his gaunt frame. His cheeks were hollow and pale, but his blue eyes smiled comradely at me as he hitched his belt tighter.

"For goodness' sake, Jorrie, how much did you lose?" I fussed over him.

"'Bout thirty pounds. But I'll pick it up fast, Doc says. Say, he's one swell guy. You know, I don't smoke anymore. Don't think I will again. Doc says my lungs'll be better off without it. Kinda hard on those beefy old lungs right now, I guess. I may even take his advice about hard booze too. Bad for the ticker, Doc says."

He paused and looked out the window. "Say . . . uh . . . thanks for sending the kids to see me."

"I didn't have to *send* them, Jorrie. They went because they wanted to."

He turned and looked at me, then looked away. "I never knew how good it could make you feel to know somebody likes you. You feel kinda . . . oh . . ." He was gazing out of the window again.

For several seconds the only sound in the room was the ticking of the big wall clock. I did not know what to say. At last I tried to answer him. "Yes, Jorrie, I know how good it is to have friends—best thing in the world."

He turned and faced me. "And you'll never believe this, Mrs. Doig. My mother came to see me after I got pretty sick. Took me home with her when I got out of the hospital. I'm home now."

CHAPTER THIRTY-TWO

The years in Three Forks were good ones. Beverly went to second and third grades and made many friends. The older twins, although somewhat shy with adults, always had playmates around them. Our yard was big, with a swing in one of the trees and a gravelly sand pit out by the garage. From the open windows I could glance out often, see little heads bent over pails and pans of dirt and sand, see hands stirring industriously, hear the chatter of voices. Always I was aware of each one, where he or she was, what was happening.

We lived on a corner with sidewalk around two sides. The street stopped at our house—out at the edge of town. There was almost no traffic. In such a small town almost everyone walked to the stores, to the post office, to school.

The children took turns riding our old tricycle along the sidewalk, into the garage, around, and back. Beverly tried to learn to ride the bike my brother left with us when he went to the Army.

Posie was one little girl who came every day. She was the same age as Margie and Marilyn. I often said to myself, "She's like the cat; we let her in in the morning and put her out at night." Her mother and father had been divorced, and she lived with a grandmother who seemed to show no interest in, or concern for, the child. Posie was never troublesome, and the older twins "mothered" her.

Beverly's friends were tomboys, playing cowboy and Indians, chasing each other around the garage, usually followed by Bo, who barked happily. He loved the children, and they thought of him almost as a person. Big and strong, he allowed himself to be ridden and crawled over. When he became tired of their nonsense, he just lay down and pretended to be asleep. Everywhere they went, however, he was with them.

On rainy days, or cold snowy ones, the children played downstairs in the basement. It was a big space with plenty of places for them to hide and room to romp and run the tricycle. Windows all around made it bright enough except on gray days when we had to use the lights. An old iron cookstove stood there, connected to the regular chimney. Here, in the summer, I did my canning where it was cool and pleasant. With joy I watched the shelves fill with rows of glass jars of food.

One little boy who often came to our yard was a trouble-maker. Timmy would pull the pansies up by the roots and throw them at the little girls. When the mother cat ventured out of the garage, he threw sticks and rocks at her. One day he picked up one of the little kittens, held it by the hind legs and beat its head against the garage until it was dead. The girls cried for hours.

I tried to talk to the little boy. He just stood and looked at me, not a sign of emotion on his face. A number of times—when we were gone—he sneaked over and cut the swing rope. I repaired it, but I wondered at the sadistic temperament of this little boy. Then I learned about his home.

Once he came into our house, while we were away, went upstairs and into the bedrooms. He took down from the wall a Boy Scout knot collection (left there by the owners of the house), tore off some of the specimens, and took them home with him. When I found out what he had done, I stomped down the block to the home of Timmy. Trying to figure out what to say, I stood knocking on the kitchen door.

Someone said, "Come in," and I did.

At the table sat a shirtless, unshaven man with a beer can tipped up to his mouth.

"You're Timmy's father?"

"His mother claims I am."

"Well, Timmy came to our house and took some things and I want them back," I said, all in one breath, then added, "I'm Mrs. Doig—I live across and down the street."

With a bang the man let the front legs of the chair down onto the floor.

"Hey, Timmy ain't no thief."

"He took the things—some Boy Scout knots," I insisted. "He even admitted it to me and then ran here. Ask him."

"Allie, come here," he bellowed.

"What do you want with me?" came a voice from another room.

"Come here, I said. Do yuh hear me?"

A woman I recognized as Timmy's mother stood in the doorway beyond the table.

"Has your little brat come home? This woman here says he took something from her house."

She disappeared and came back in a few moments with both hands full of the knots. She threw them on the floor in front of me. I picked them up and backed out of the house, mumbling something. I was still angry.

For a few days Timmy did not come to our house. But before long he was there again. I always watched him carefully after that.

Another little boy—this one named Scott, the exact age of the younger twins—was a favorite of the children's. He was polite and played happily with them. Sometimes he would invite Jimmy and Joan to his yard and share turns riding in his shiny new car. When he ran into his house for a cookie, he brought back one for each of the twins too.

One day I looked up from my sewing and noted that Jimmy was missing from the yard, but not Joan. This was unusual. I called through the open window, "Where's Jimmy?"

"Oh, he went with Scott," Beverly answered. "Scotty's mother said he had to take a bath and invited Jimmy to come in and talk to Scott while he is in the tub."

It was story time before I was reminded of the incident again. In the middle of the story I was reading, Jimmy called out, "Mom, I went to Scott's house today."

"Yes, I know you did," I said and went on reading the story.

"Mom," Jimmy interrupted again, "I saw Scott take a bath. And Mom, he's made just like me, not like the girls. I'm a boy like him, huh, Mom?"

"Yes, Jimmy," I said. "You're a boy; you're different from a girl. Some day you'll be a man like your daddy."

"And like Scotty's daddy too?"

I hadn't realized how it had seemed to him—this one little male among all of us females. Poor little fellow! He must have wondered about this many times!

I went on to finish reading the bedtime story.

CHAPTER THIRTY-THREE

Junior prom was a very important occasion in this little town. It was a community affair. Not only members of the upper classes in the high school and their dates attended; all adults in Three Forks were invited to come if they paid their dollar and a half at the door. Spectator tickets, sold for fifty cents, allowed visitors to go up in the balcony and watch the whole evening's activities. It was a formal festivity. Dresses were almost to the floor, and those males who could rented white jackets. Even older couples came and waltzed sedately while the younger ones were doing the newer dances.

The gymnasium was transformed into a bower of artificial flowers, made of crepe paper, with colorful streamers hiding the metal trusses of the ceiling. Juniors worked late into the nights twisting and tacking the strips of paper, cutting stars from cardboard, smearing them with glue, sprinkling them silver, suspending them below the blue canopy of imitation sky.

Holland was the theme of the prom that year. A huge windmill, constructed by the shop classes, had been placed at each end of the gym to hide the basketball rings. The junior girls chattered and giggled as they cut pieces of red and yellow paper and formed tulips. Four sophomore girls, chosen to serve the punch, studied pictures of old Dutch costumes. All of the home economics sewing classes helped to plan and sew and fit the quaint dresses and caps and aprons for the costumes. The whole school was agog with the excitement of preparation.

In our house there was a buzz of excitement too. As

adviser of the senior class, of course, I had been invited. My youngest sister had sent me her formal—a blue taffeta that reached almost to my toes. Then early in April the junior class voted to ask my older twins to act as flower girls for the queen. When the written invitation came, addressed to Margie and Marilyn, I read it aloud and waited for the reaction. No one said anything. I began to explain what this meant. The twins' eyes grew big with wonder. Shy as they had always been, I wondered whether they would gain confidence enough, even with much practicing, to walk down the full length of the gym with so many eyes on them. Gradually the importance of the invitation and the delight of becoming part of the prom took hold of each little girl.

"It's something like when I was a flower girl for Auntie Irene, isn't it, Mother?" said Beverly. "At first I was scared, but it was really fun."

Getting ready for this was a family affair. First we talked about dresses. In Bozeman we bought white organdy and pink ribbon. We looked at white shoes, priced them. I shook my head, explaining to the children why we could not afford them.

On the way home we stopped at Anna's, and she helped me cut out the material. The dresses would be really formal—all the way to the floor, with ruffles around the bottom. With two of us basting and sewing and fitting, the dresses were rapidly put together. Bundling everything under my arm, I shooed the children into the car.

"I can finish them in my odd minutes," I said.

"But there should be white shoes to go with them," Anna said, her hand on the car window as I started the engine.

"I know, but I can't quite manage that." We went on home.

During the next two weeks the dresses were completed.

Beverly helped me tie the bows of pink ribbon and space them on the ruffles.

"Now hold two fingers straight up, like so," I said and guided her hands to a position for tying the big pink bow that would be fastened at the front of each dress, the long ends of ribbon dropping all the way to the bottom. With hands held firmly, Beverly watched as I wrapped the ribbon and tied it between her upraised fingers. Two of these we made, then two short bows to put on the twins' hair.

The prom was always held on Saturday. All of that exciting day I kept trying to remind the twins of the do's and do not's. In the practice the evening before, they had walked so solemnly across the gym floor.

"Try to remember to smile as you walk along."

"Like this?" Margie asked as she pulled her face up into an unnatural grimace.

"Oh, no," Beverly said as she shook her head.

"But how then?" Marilyn asked.

"Well, think of something very happy. Let's see—oh, I know. Remember how you felt when you found our baby kittens last week? Think about that as you march."

"And don't stare just straight ahead. Turn to the right and left a little, just your head, so everyone can see your smile."

We practiced promenading up and down the living room as I played a march on the piano. I wanted to say, "Try not to let your old shoes show," but that would make them more self-conscious of them. Silently I mourned for white ones.

"Girls, I hear the mailman out on the porch. Why don't you go to see if there's a letter from Grandma or Uncle Kenneth?"

There was a scurry to see who could get there first, and

then I heard squeals of delight as they came running back into the house.

"A package, Mother, a package! Did you send for something in the catalog?"

"No," I answered, looking for the return address. "Oh, it's from Auntie Anna. Run get the scissors and cut the string."

Again a scuffle to be first to the sewing machine drawer, and then the fumbling of string and paper. When the package lay opened, the astonishment made them catch their breath for a second. Then there were cries of joy.

"White shoes," Margie said.

"Two pairs," Marilyn echoed. "Must be for us twins. Oh, to wear with our white dresses tonight!"

There they lay—four shiny little white patent leather slippers. I felt that I had never seen anything so beautiful in my life. Margie and Marilyn grabbed the shoes up in their arms and danced around the room.

"They're so pretty," I said putting my arms around Beverly. "We are happy for them, aren't we, dear?"

Beverly nodded. "I'm glad. I didn't want to be ashamed of the old ones."

"Try them on," I suggested. No one even dared to think of such a foolish idea as their not fitting. I should have known that Anna knew their size. She had shopped with us for shoes many times.

The prom was a triumph for us all. Guarded by Beverly, Jimmy and Joan leaned over the balustrade of the balcony and watched every move of the procession. My eyes were only on a pair of six-year-old girls, dressed in white organdy, carrying pink roses, and wearing shiny white slippers which peeped out from under the gowns at each step.

CHAPTER THIRTY-FOUR

I was ironing in the dining room the summer day that the telegram came. The unaccustomed peal of the doorbell sent me hurrying through the living room and the front hall. At the door stood my neighbor and the Western Union boy. Holding the door open, I took the yellow envelope held out to me as my neighbor entered the hall and stood beside me. The Western Union messenger touched his hat and left. I tore open the envelope and read the short message in one glance. "Kenneth missing in action. Plane shot down over Hungary." It was signed "Mother."

For a moment I stood there, devoid of feeling. Only one thing penetrated my consciousness for a few minutes: the rays of the sun that had been so warm a short time ago now seemed cold. Then I began to feel the tears sliding down over my face. My neighbor put her arm about my shoulders.

"He asked me to come with him—the Western Union boy. I didn't know just what was in the message," she said.

I handed her the telegram. She read it silently.

"Was this the brother who became a pilot?" she asked.

"No, the navigator, my baby brother. I took more care of him than my mother did when he was little. I was with him in Boise, Idaho, in April, just before he went overseas."

The children came in and stood looking at us. I tried to explain, without frightening them, the cause of my tears.

"He may be a prisoner; we don't know. You know about the parachutes that are worn by our men in airplanes, don't you?"

I had gained my composure. My neighbor left. Mechanically I went back to the ironing, finding some comfort in physical work. As I swept the iron back and forth across the starched dresses, I tried to think what I could do for Mother. I decided to send a night letter and began to compose one as I finished the ironing.

With the children I walked downtown to the Western Union office where I put onto the yellow sheet handed me there the words of comfort I had thought out. An answer came next day, a telegram from my brother Sam. He was with Mother, who had had a light heart attack and was resting now. He would stay there with her until she was better.

In a few weeks Mother began to get letters from the parents of the other members of the crew, telling of their sons writing from prison camps in Hungary. Only the bombardier and Kenneth did not write. The months went by, and we tried to encourage Mother by writing that some of the men who were in war in prison could not get letters out, but were still alive. At Christmastime I persuaded her to come to stay with us for two weeks. When I met her train, I did not recognize her at first. She had lost forty pounds. Her face was thin, and her hair was white. The visit may have helped, but she was restless, thinking that a letter might be sent to her home and she would not be there to get it. I quit trying to hold her with me.

V-E Day was a joyful event for most people. For us, it was a dubious one. Prisoners soon began to be released and return to the United States. Still no word came from Kenneth. The certainty that he was not alive began to fix itself in my mind. When Mother became sure of this, would her heart stand the strain? She was alone. None of us even lived near her. She would not leave, would not come to live with any of us. Here I was—footloose; school was almost out. Why not live near Mother and teach in

Missouri? My children should gain much from being near their grandmother.

Teaching positions were plentiful everywhere because of the war. I liked Three Forks, and salaries were so much better in Montana than in Missouri, yet I felt I owed much to my mother.

By mail I found a position in a high school near her home; I planned to move as soon as school was out. Eight-year-old Beverly and I put every piece of furniture that we planned to take with us in the two-car garage until the moving van could come—everything except the piano and the refrigerator, that is. How we ever carried that washing machine up those crooked stairs from the basement I'll never know.

The car was now nine years old. The tires were smooth, and new ones could not be bought. I would have to make out with what I had. Using all my persuasive power— "tears in my eyes and my fists doubled up," I always called it—I secured gas stamps enough to make the thirteen-hundred-mile journey to Missouri.

The first night we stopped at my brother-in-law's ranch near Big Timber. The children scampered out of the car and ran to see their cousins. Claude looked at the old tires, walked around the car, sized up my load, and groaned.

"Elsie, you can never make it with those old tires. You better stick around awhile. I'll see what I can do with our ration board." He pushed his hat to the back of his head and hitched up his Levis as he walked around the car again.

"I have an extra one in the trunk. Not much better, but at least it's a spare," I explained. The children came back all talking at once.

"Mother, they have two little colts and ten bum lambs. Can we help feed the lambs tonight?"

"Sure thing," Claude answered them. "Hey, Sonny," he called to his boy, "why don't you saddle a gentle horse and take the kids for a ride?"

The girls followed Sonny to the barn. Only Jimmy took hold of my hand. He was still afraid to climb up on objects—afraid of heights—so insecure in any unaccustomed physical action. We were just beginning to realize how handicapped he really was.

Seeing his withdrawal, Claude held out his hand. "You can ride in the saddle with me. I'll hold on to you." Jimmy let go my hand and took his uncle's outstretched one.

The evening was filled with excitement. Dora, the children's aunt, and I cooked supper and caught up on news of the Doig families. After supper we talked until late. Then Dora took us to the bunkhouse which she had cleaned and put fresh bedding on the beds. After the children were asleep I was on my knees a long time talking to the Lord about this trip. If ever anyone needed a guardian, it was I.

We were on the road next morning long before sunup. The children went back to sleep and I drove alone—it seemed to me—along the Yellowstone River. "Must not drive fast," I warned myself often. "Those tires are so thin. Besides there's a government rule—not over thirty-five miles an hour during war time." Scraps of old songs came to my mind, and I sang softly to myself. Beverly was the first to awaken.

"Mother, I wasn't afraid to sleep in the bunkhouse last night. It was fun. But there was a little mouse in the corner. Marilyn screamed when it came close to her bed. A mouse wouldn't hurt her, would it, Mother?"

"No, dear."

The others awakened and began to get restless.

"Beverly, up above the back seat is a brown paper sack.

Remember? Open it and take out a pair of little scissors for each of you. Now take the big catalog and find a page of little boys for Jim and one of little girls for Joan and the other twins. Can you find those old scrapbooks on the floor? Let's make up some stories for those little girls and boys as you paste them in the books."

This lasted awhile, and then they needed a diversion. We stopped at a service station and got some gas. Each one had a drink of water and a trip to the rest room. Back in the car, we found the color books this time.

At noon we stopped beside the Wind River in Wyoming. While the youngsters took off their shoes and stockings and waded in the clear water I unpacked the lunch and spread it out on newspapers under a big aspen tree. We ate with the usual enthusiasm. We had a saying in our family: "When Mother calls supper, we all run; if anyone stumbles on the way that one finds little to eat when he gets to the table!" No sweeping up crumbs this time! The pine squirrels and birds would do it for me.

On our way again, the twins' chattering soon stopped as they leaned against the seats and slept. Beverly sat in front with me now and held the map. As we traveled I explained to her how to read to me the names of the towns along our road. When the children wakened, the older ones played the game of spelling out the alphabet by getting letters from advertising signs. It took all my ingenuity to provide interesting activities for them.

That night we had a room in a little hotel. Rooms to rent were still scarce, even for just one night, because of the people moving across the country to work in munitions plants and other war-product factories. Six of us slept in one little room! I spread quilts on the floor for Beverly and the older twins. Jim, Joan, and I had the big bed. It had been a long day, but I couldn't go to sleep. My shoulders and neck ached from the hours of driving and the tension.

"Why pull up all roots and move so far away?" The question nagged at my mind. I dragged out all my threadbare answers, but none seemed to satisfy me. I was afraid and insecure now; I wanted to go back to Montana.

"Mother, I'm cold. I haven't any covers," Joan whispered from her side of the bed.

After I had tucked the quilt around her, I took myself in hand. "Now, look here," I said, "you have made your decision. You have prayed and prayed about it. It seemed the best thing to do. You've burned your bridges behind you. The only way you can go is straight ahead." But I turned and tossed restlessly most of the night.

About four in the morning it was beginning to get daylight. I carried the still sleeping twins out to the car. Beverly dressed and helped me load the quilts and the suitcase. As I drove along in the cool morning, there was complete silence in the car. Even Beverly had gone back to sleep. The roads were free from traffic and the tires were cool, so I could drive a little faster.

That day and the next were long and tiresome. The air became hot and humid, and we were sweaty and tired as we drove into Mother's yard the next afternoon.

Grandma tried to put her arms around all the children at once as she welcomed them. They followed her into the house for cookies and milk, then out to the barnyard to see the little calf and the chickens. I sank down on the davenport and fell asleep. It must have been an hour before the children's voices awakened me.

The next morning I drove downtown to see a real estate man about finding a house I could buy. Near the middle of town I had to drive across the railroad tracks. I noticed the signalman standing with the train flag in his hand. Suddenly I was aware that my steering wheel had no control over guiding the car. I pushed on the brake pedal and stopped.

"Hey, you, come on! There's a train coming," shouted the signalman.

"I can't. My car won't steer," I yelled. I saw the signalman run to two fellows standing nearby and shout and point. The three men came quickly to my car.

"Take it out of gear," they said as they began to push the car across the tracks. In a few moments we were in a safe place and the fast passenger train screamed past. For a minute I could not think clearly. Then I got awkwardly out of the car and went to call for a wrecker to pull my car to a garage. I stood speechless until the wrecker came; the driver looked under my car and shook his head.

"Tie rods all disconnected—broken or worn out, don't know which yet. You're lucky you're alive," he said.

I didn't answer. I thought of the miles of mountain roads I had just traveled and said silently, "Thank you, God, for your protection. I really needed that guardian angel, didn't I?"

CHAPTER THIRTY-FIVE

We arrived in Missouri in the last of May. For a few weeks we settled down in my mother's home while I searched for a house to buy. A large air base ten miles away made housing scarce. Margie learned to milk Grandma's cow. Marilyn liked feeding the chickens. Beverly considered herself errand girl.

Then it began to rain. For days the rain continued. Five active children cooped up in a house can make even a mother feel like climbing the walls. For Grandmother, accustomed to the quiet of just herself and her little dog, it became a distraction. Even the dog got cross and tried to bite Jimmy.

One day I found a temporary solution. Putting on coats and old overshoes, the children and I sloshed down to the barn. We climbed a ladder to a miniature haymow; there we played games, told stories, and wore out the accumulated tension of living in a house that was not our own—where we had to be quiet, to be careful not to bump into or break anything. Up in the barn loft, we could romp and play, make noise, enjoy the activity that is a part of the animal life of small children.

When the sun shone again, I began to call real estate agencies once more, trying to find a house for sale that did not cost too much. The banker at home in Montana had told me he thought he could sell our house in Manhattan. He wrote me, about a week after we had arrived in Missouri, that he had an offer of $2,500. Immediately I told him to accept and sell for me.

Then the letters came from the crew members of my

brother's plane. The first one convinced me, but Mother would not accept it. "Kenneth was badly wounded by flak," the copilot wrote. "I helped him put on his parachute and I think he landed safely, but he wasn't in prison with us. I'm sure he's dead."

The pilot's letter came the next day. I read it slowly aloud to Mother. "Kenneth landed not far from me. He was dazed from his wounds, and the Hungary military shot him and the bombardier. I don't know why unless it was because of his wounded condition. They bragged about it as they took us to prison."

Mother began to cry and moan. I called the doctor. By the time he arrived, she was unconscious. He muttered some words. I caught one—"coronary," and interpreted to myself—another heart attack. My brother Sammy was about a hundred miles away. He came and helped me care for her.

The children and their need of her were the only concepts that she held onto for those first few days. Gradually she regained her strength. But I knew that my brood of five must not live with her all the time—just be near her.

I resumed my hunting for a house. I found one for sale just four blocks away. It was not pretentious, but I could buy it. A few days later a check came from the bank in Montana. Our house there had been sold. Here was the money—$2,500. I looked at it and for the first time in several years I was filled with awe—this was exactly the amount that I would need to pay for the house we had been contemplating buying. I called the real estate man and closed the deal.

The next day the children and I walked over to the little house we had bought. I turned the key in the lock, and we went in through the back door. The hot, musty odor was almost nauseating. I began to open windows as

I talked excitedly to the children about "our new home." They did not respond.

"Plenty of space in the kitchen here for us to have a table so we can eat in this room."

No one said anything.

"That's the bathroom," I said as I opened the door to a small, empty room.

"There's nothing there," Beverly said solemnly.

"We'll have a new bathtub and stool and washbowl put in right away. Just think—a brand new bathroom." But they showed no enthusiasm. We went into the dining room.

"Four big windows! This will be a good place to play and to work." I let the blinds spring up, bringing in a flood of light. "I'll put my sewing machine by these west windows."

The living room was darker because the windows were shaded by big trees near the south side of the house. Into the bedroom we went, exploring everything, up the narrow, steep stairs to the bedrooms on the second floor. Here the hot air was stifling. With difficulty I raised the windows to let fresh air blow through, then went back downstairs. Quietly, obediently, the children followed me out into the backyard; no one was even interested enough to ask questions.

"Beverly, can you bring me that rope in the trunk of the car?" I started for a great cottonwood tree that reached much higher than the house.

Beverly came, dragging the rope. I threw one end of it over a big branch about twelve feet above me, made a slip knot, and pulled the rope tight. "Here—you kids can run and swing by your feet until I get that old ladder I saw in the weeds behind the garage."

One of the twins took the end of the rope, stood there

looking up at the end tied to the branch. Bringing the ladder to the trunk of the tree, I climbed to the place where the big branch joined the trunk. Cautiously I crawled out on the branch until I reached the knot of the rope fastened there.

"Throw me the other end of the rope," I called.

Marilyn and Margie each tried but failed each time.

"Here, let me," Beverly said. After two attempts she managed to lob the end of the rope over the branch near my reaching hands. I tied this end of the rope tightly around the branch, about eighteen inches from the other knot, and edged my way to the ladder and down to the ground.

"Now, let's see if the rope is too long. You try to sit in it, Joan. We want it low enough for you to swing." Her bottom touched the ground as she sat in the loop of rope.

"Too low, Mother," Beverly decided. I was glad for any enthusiasm or interest.

"Well, I'll tie a knot in it, to take up some of the length. Somebody get the hatchet out of the car. We'll find a piece of board and make a seat. Margie, can you get the hatchet? Come on, Marilyn, help me find a board. You know, about so long. There are all sorts of things in the garage."

We put the key in the padlock on the garage doors. The rusty lock opened with difficulty. We kicked at some boards until we found one just the right length. I notched the ends of it and took it to the rope swing.

"Me first," Jim said.

I lifted him to the seat and began to push him gently. He was always afraid to go high. I could feel him tighten his hands on the rope, but he wanted to do the things the others did.

"Mother, I need to go to the bathroom. Can I go to the

little toilet out there in the corner of the yard?" Margie asked.

"Yes, Margie. It's just like Grandma's. You'll be all right, won't you?"

"I guess so. Come with me, Marilyn."

Idly I pushed Jim and looked over the yard. It did seem discouraging, getting any interest in this house—for the children at least. Suddenly I heard a scream and turned to see Margie running out of the toilet, brushing her arms and face as she ran.

"Hornets," Marilyn cried, running too.

We could see the hornets leave Margie and circle, but she cried frenziedly and held her arm for me to see a welt rapidly becoming pink and bruised-looking. I ran to turn on the water at the outside hydrant, made some mud which I put on the red welt. Margie sobbed, her shoulders heaving, the tears streaming. She was scared as well as hurt. The hornets had not stung Marilyn, but she was scared too.

"Let's go back to Grandma's," she begged.

After dark that night, I took my big flashlight, a can of kerosene, several matches, and a can of insect spray. Alone I walked to the house we had just bought and out to the little toilet. Spraying the insect poison around as I entered, I soon found, by flashing my light, the big hornet's nest in one corner of the deep hole beneath. I poured kerosene into the nest, dropped burning pieces of paper onto the kerosene. Fire flared up, followed by a dull buzzing of the drugged hornets. I stayed there until everything was quiet and the fire was out.

Early next morning I went back to look at the hornets' nest. I could hear nothing, could see only dead hornets, but again I squirted insect spray over everything.

Later in the day with boxes of kalsomine and brushes and

buckets I returned to the house. The children asked to stay with Grandma. For hours I worked in one of the upstairs bedrooms, putting a coat of pale yellow paint on the walls and ceiling, making it look clean and fresh. It was so hot I had stripped to my panties and bra. I scrubbed the floors, the windows, the windowsills. The air smelled of paint, but the musty, stale odor was gone. I washed my brushes and returned to Mother's house.

Each day I scrubbed and cleaned. Then I put up curtains at the shining windows and clean paper on the shelves. Our furniture arrived at the end of the week. The big truck drove up before the door of my mother's house. When the driver got out of the cab he called to me, "You Mrs. Doig?"

"Yes."

"I need two hundred forty dollars and forty-five cents in cash before I can unload your furniture," he said as he took off his cap and pushed back his sweaty hair.

"In cash? I can give you a check."

"Can't take no check. Company says cash!"

"I can get it in the morning—oh, no, tomorrow's Sunday. Will you give me a few minutes to see what I can do?"

He nodded, leaned against the truck, and took out a cigarette. I went into the house so puzzled that I could not think what to do.

"Call the chief of police," Mother suggested. "No, maybe I'd better do it. He's a very good friend of mine. He can go to a bar or beer joint and get the cash for us."

She took the receiver off the hook and began to talk to the operator, and then to the police chief.

"He'll get the money," she said as she put back the receiver. "I told him to meet us at your new house. Now let's get the trucker to take the load of furniture over there."

She went with me to the furniture van and then to my

car. We followed the big truck to the "new" house. In about twenty minutes the police car drove up and the chief squeezed his huge bulk from under the steering wheel. In exchange for the handful of bills he held out to me, I gave him my check, thanked him, and took the money to the trucker and watched him count it carefully. Not until the trucker had folded the bills with his dirty hands and put them in his billfold did he even unlock the back of the truck and begin to take out the furniture.

It was dark before we finished carrying all our belongings into the house. The next day the children came with me to the house. Somehow, just seeing their own familiar things in the rooms gave them the sense of home. They began to accept the house now and chattered over the shiny new faucets which had been put in the bathroom the day before. Jim and Joan ran up and down the stairs, in and out of the house, swinging under the big cottonwood tree, finding a pile of dirt near there in which they could play. Beverly helped me push and lift furniture into place. The older twins began to unpack pans and dishes and put them into the cupboards. By evening we were sweaty and dirty but settled. We washed and dried on "our own towels."

"Anybody want to go with me to buy groceries?" I called, looking for my purse. "I know a store that is open until late." I did not need an answer as the children hurried to the car.

Buying groceries was always fun. We went up and down the aisles, filling our grocery cart. At our house again it was good to put food on the shelves in the kitchen, to fill the refrigerator, to make ready for living here. A trip to Grandma's house for our clothes, and we were ready to stay in our new house. After we had our story time I played the familiar songs on the old piano while the children went to sleep. It was home.

We settled down to a summer routine. Grandma had a little garden and a big black and white Holstein cow. The girls enjoyed measuring out the pail of ground grain for her and pouring it in front of her sniffing nose. Her pasture was just below the barn, down to the spring, and up the hill to the other fence—acres of it. Grandma took us to a big thicket of blackberries, and we picked them when they were ripe. The thorns on these bushes tore at our clothes and made deep scratches on our hands, but the berries were large and juicy. We picked them in the early morning before the heat of the sun became unbearable. In the afternoons I canned the berries and baked succulent cobblers.

In August I enrolled the three older girls in the college laboratory school which was just a few blocks away: Beverly in the fourth grade, the older twins in the second. Jim and Joan were enrolled in the kindergarten. To get to the school the children walked just a block to the college stadium, across the football field, and onto the campus. There was no traffic to worry about. In the afternoon, the younger twins stayed at Grandma's house, except for Thursday and Friday when Mrs. Coop came to our house to do our washing and ironing.

About a month after school began something happened that I knew nothing about until it was all over. One night after supper, as we cleared the table and washed the dishes, Beverly said calmly, "Well, Mother, Margie and Marilyn took care of that for you."

"Took care of what?" I stopped with my hands full of plates on my way to the sink.

"Oh, three big boys have been laying for Jimmy every night and pestering him. Sometimes they beat him up."

"Beverly, why didn't you tell me?"

"We didn't want to worry you."

"Oh, dear!" I felt so inadequate, trying to hold down two jobs—at home, at work—neglecting my family.

"It's all right now. The twins—Margie and Marilyn, I mean—were out at eleven thirty today, you know. They hurried down to the stadium where they hid and waited. They saw Jim and Joan coming, then the mean boys. Margie and Marilyn jumped onto the boys, shook 'em up, and told 'em they'd beat the tar out of them if they didn't let Jim alone. The boys hollered and bawled and ran away. I don't think they'll try it again." And that solved it—for a while at least.

Now my kids were helping me solve my problems.

CHAPTER THIRTY-SIX

One morning, soon after I arrived in Missouri, Mother said to me, "Elsie, why don't you take some courses at the college this summer? It's so near. How many credits do you need to finish your master's degree? You have almost enough graduate work, don't you? It will take time for those men to finish putting in your sewage system and your bathroom so that you can move into your house. The children will be with me. Even after you do get into your own home, you can send them here while you attend classes. After summer school is over I can help you with your sewing for the children's school year."

We talked about this for a while, but I did not need to be convinced. Searching through my special papers, I found a copy of my college transcript, counted graduate credits. I had taken my undergraduate work with this college and had obtained a bachelor's degree, so I did not need to have transfer of those credits. Next morning I made an appointment with the dean of the graduate school. I needed only a few semester hours. These I could earn during the summer session.

In a few days I was enrolled in the college and had made application for my master's degree. My classes were early in the morning. Afternoons I studied out in the yard where the children played. Evenings and late into the night I pored over texts, wrote research papers, took notes. When it was very hot, I cooled my feet in a tub of cold water, my head with a wet towel. It was hard work, but at the end of the summer's work, I learned something about praying and gained a concept of the real purpose of education.

In my field, before I was finally accepted as a candidate for graduation, I had to pass an oral examination—go before a board of faculty members from the departments in which I had studied and answer any questions that these dignitaries might give me. A date was set for this examination; the members were chosen to do the questioning. The time drew near, and I began to be afraid.

I reviewed from old textbooks, studied rules and facts. It had been many years since I had begun college. I had forgotten so much of what I was supposed to know. How could I answer questions about the history of education, about the schools of the state, about—oh, any number of things? I was filled with worry.

"They're toughening up on the graduate school candidates this year," I heard again and again. Then one day as I went down the hall, the door of the conference room was suddenly flung open and a teacher-friend of mine rushed out. As she passed me I had a glimpse of tears running down her face. Later I heard that her board had failed to pass her, and she was told she would have to try again next year.

Panic mounted within me. This woman was a good teacher, I had heard—calm, competent. What would I do under severe questioning?

The evening before my orals I was too worried to eat. For weeks I had been praying about this ordeal. That night as I dropped to my knees beside my bed I began to pray aloud. Suddenly I realized what I was saying, what I had been saying all the time: "Lord, make me smart enough! Help me not to be dumb! Please, Lord, let me know the answers." And then all at once I knew that this was not what I should be praying—not this "gimme" talk; this was not communion with God. I began to understand what I really should be talking to him about.

"Lord, please let me reflect thy teachings as I answer those questions tomorrow. Let me show that I can be a good teacher because a knowledge of thee has helped me to know a better way of life. Help me to let my light shine. . . . Several of these men on my board know of my religious convictions. They have known me. I have studied in their classes."

Oh, I knew of the omniscience of God, but *I* was made aware of all these things as I attempted to commune with Him. And I continued, "Please, dear Lord, help me to forget myself. Help me to glorify thy name as I answer the questions."

The next morning I went very early to the education building and waited near the door of the conference room. There was an inside entrance into the room, also. At the exact time appointed, I went in. Five men were already seated around the large table. Another one came in from the inner door as I sat down. They all smiled and spoke to me, calling me by name.

With no preliminaries, the head of the education department turned to Mr. G. of the English department and said, "Would you like to question her first?"

My heart beat very fast. My breathing was shallow and rapid. And then a strange thing happened. I felt a warm glow in the region of my heart. My fear just seemed to flow away. I felt good.

"Mrs. Doig, how would you teach Wordsworth?"

"I'm glad you chose Wordsworth," I said. "I often begin with his poem, 'We Are Seven.' It's in most anthologies for senior English. First I would ask the students questions something like this: What is death? What do you know about death? How would you explain death to a child? When I begin to feel that the students are interested, begin

to get responses, I tell them—with no show of emotion—
that I had to explain to my children when their father died,
and I found it very difficult to know what to say. There had
been seven of us—my husband and I and the five children;
then he was gone and there were no longer seven. Then I
would read the poem to the class:

> . . . a simple child,
> That lightly draws its breath,
> And feels its life in every limb,
> What should it know of death?
>
> I met a little cottage girl:
> She was eight years old, she said;
> Her hair was thick with many a curl
> That clustered round her head.

And on to the last lines:

> 'Twas throwing words away; for still
> The little maid would have her will,
> And said, Nay, we are seven!

I feel the students thinking with me as I read. I do not
need to explain the poem after I have finished reading it.

"Then probably I would go on to 'The World Is Too
Much with Us,'" I said. "To establish rapport for this one
I often begin to talk about going hunting, fishing, hiking,
camping out in the open—getting away from the noise and
confusion of urban life. When the students begin to respond freely, when I get them with me, I read

> The world is too much with us; late and soon,
> Getting and spending, we lay waste our powers:
> Little we see in Nature that is ours;
> We have given our hearts away, a sordid boon. . . .

Mr. G. was leaning back in his chair, listening and nodding his head. The other five men seemed interested.

"Now, Mrs. Doig," he said, "how about teaching Burns?"

This was just as easy. I began with "A Man's a Man for A' That," but—as before—I explained how I would lay a foundation for the students to have an experience with me as I read the poem—for them to gain new insights, new concepts of life, new understandings of people and situations.

"It's my turn," interrupted the chairman of the education department. "What would you do with a student who couldn't write, one who was an F student?"

"I'm sure I have made all the mistakes in the catalog, but I try very hard to find out about my students—I try to understand them—so I can teach them. For instance, a few years ago I had one fellow who couldn't grasp even the simple fundamentals of grammar, couldn't write, couldn't spell. At first I felt that he was hopeless. But gradually, from his essays, from little scraps of conversation that I happened to overhear, from his responses to questions, I learned of his background. His mother had died when he was small. His father was a bartender. The boy grew up in a saloon, took his naps under the counter, helped to carry out the bottles, learned the language of the people who frequent the bar.

"And then I had a glimpse of his acuity when, as we made up metaphors in class one day, he wrote, 'I shot my deer through his engine room.' True, it was crude, and he had misspelled three words in the sentence, but I made sure that, after the spelling had been changed, this example of a figure of speech was included in our school literary magazine that month.

"When the time came for research papers to be written, he stopped after school to see me. His face reflected his consternation.

" 'Mrs. Doig, I can't write a paper six pages long—you know that.'

" 'Well, let's see,' I said. 'What do you really like best?' I was fumbling for an idea, I knew, but when he answered, 'Cars,' I grabbed onto the subject. I remembered the time I had happened into the auto mechanics shop during the class period and he had emerged from beneath an old jalopy to explain to me all about the 'innards' of his car.

" 'Your car. You can write something about cars.' And we were off to a start.

"Weeks later his essay came in on time. A treatise on the electrical connections in cars, it was not of much literary value, but he had made wooden covers for the paper—front and back pieces—had sanded the rounded corners until they were symmetrical, had varnished the wood to a glossy surface, had wired a spark plug to the top cover.

" 'Someone helped me proof it,' he admitted ruefully as he laid it on my desk."

"Don't I get a chance to question?" asked one member of the counseling department, as I paused for a moment. His question was about some intricate detail of a new test we had been giving that summer to some college students who had served as experiments for intern counseling. For a second or two I could not remember the details, and then again the warm feeling returned and I was able to relax and give a satisfactory answer.

The minutes went by rapidly. Several times one of my questioners said, "I know we should go on to our classes, but I want to ask another question."

More than two hours passed before they dismissed me, and I let myself out of the room and went to the library to study.

The next morning as I walked to my nine o'clock class, a fellow classmate of mine caught up with me and began to talk excitedly.

"Say, Elsie, what do you think Mr. F. talked about in our eight o'clock class just now? You! Oh, he didn't mention your name, but he said it was a teacher who had been taking her orals yesterday morning, and I knew the time of your appointment. He said that this person was the kind of teacher we want in our classrooms, that she reflected the ideals students should know and understand."

I did not answer—I could not. The bell rang as we slid into our seats in the classroom. I did not hear the first few minutes of the lecture. I was busy communing with my Master. I was thanking Him for letting me have this experience, for helping me to understand that education is not for ostentation, not for display. I was thanking Him for giving me this new concept of teaching, for helping me to see how my vocation could fit into the work of the Master. I was thanking Him for helping me to learn how to pray.

CHAPTER THIRTY-SEVEN

Margie and Marilyn were eight years old in July that year. In June they had watched with eager eyes the baptisms of other boys and girls whose eighth birthday had come before Children's Day.

"Mother, will we have to wait until next year to be baptized? That's a long time."

"No, I think we'll find a way before then. Let's see now—there's our church reunion at Gardner Lake next week. We can't afford to go the whole week, but we could drive there for one day. Often there are baptisms in the lake during reunion. I'll ask our pastor about it right away."

After several attempts, I was able to talk to him over the telephone. He promised to let me know what could be done. Saturday he called.

"Mrs. Doig, I've made the arrangements. We'll perform the baptism for the twins Thursday evening at Gardner Lake. Have you any request about who will officiate?"

"We don't know many people yet," I said. "It'll be okay if you choose."

The excitement that filled the little girls touched all six of us.

"Mother, we don't have any white dresses. Don't children always wear white for this?"

"Not always. Why can't you wear those light blue dresses that Aunt Anna made for you, the ones with the little white flowers appliqued around the skirts? Get them and we'll see if they're clean."

They were satisfied and ran to their bedroom to bring the

dresses. We washed and starched and ironed. We talked much about their coming experience.

"Mother, Beverly had to fold her hands like this." Marilyn put the palms of her hands together and linked the fingers. "Shall we do that?"

"Yes," I answered as I turned the skirt of the dress on the ironing board.

"And should we shut our eyes?" Margie asked.

"And your mouths too," Beverly explained, "and make your nose squeeze together so no water can get in."

"Will I be afraid?" Marilyn said.

"No, I think not," I assured her, looking into her wide-open eyes.

"Can we do it too?" Joan didn't want to left out.

"When you're eight years old," Beverly told her. "You're only six now."

Thursday morning we packed a box of lunch into the car, and put in a suitcase with a change of clothes for the older twins. We were dressed and ready to leave by eight o'clock.

It was over an hour's drive to the Gardner Lake reunion grounds. The children shyly stayed close to me as we entered the big tent for the first meeting. Later I took them to the activities for their own age groups. Then I relaxed and enjoyed the fellowship of the adults.

Just before sundown the campers began to wander to the lakeside, a blanket or a cushion under one arm. They sat on the ground, a gradual incline, about twenty feet back from the edge of the water. The laughter and conversation gradually ceased and we sat quietly waiting. The children and I were down in front. In the stillness, Jimmy and Joan scooted closer to me, a little diffident in the unaccustomed crowd.

Apostle Mesley came to us, took Marilyn and Margie by the hand, and led them a few feet away onto the sandy beach nearer the lake. He dropped to one knee on the ground beside them and holding a hand of each little girl he was quiet for a moment. Then he began to speak to them, but so distinctly that his words carried to the crowd on the hillside.

"Margie and Marilyn," he said, and his voice lingered on the words. "Those are beautiful names. Your mother gave them to you because she liked them and because she loved you. Now you are taking on another name—the name of Jesus Christ. This is a beautiful name, too, beautiful for what it means to us. Everything you do will show how much you love him and revere his name. When you go down into the water and are baptized, you are promising everyone that you will accept him as your Savior. You will be a member of the church which bears his name. Do you understand?"

Their heads nodded almost in unison. Apostle Mesley stood up, then led the children to the water's edge where the pastor was reaching toward them.

"Which one first?" the pastor asked.

"Me, and I'm Margie." She stepped forward. With her hand in the pastor's she walked out into the water until it was waist-deep on her. With a towel over my arm, I moved close to Marilyn. I looked out over the peaceful water. The rays of the setting sun flashed across the lake, making red reflections. It was a setting of serenity, one most appropriate for the beautiful ordinance, the ageless ceremony.

The pastor raised one hand and spoke the prayer of baptism. Tears came softly down my face. I lifted my eyes. "With your help I've come this far, Lord," I said. "Help me to go on a little farther."

There was a splash as the pastor immersed the little girl in the lake. She stood there wiping the water from her face, then walked slowly out of the water to where I waited to put a towel around her. She shivered once, and then watched as Marilyn went into the lake to be baptized.

Again the pastor walked into deeper water with a little girl by the hand and repeated the exact words of the ordinance, before lowering her into the water and bringing her out again. It was so quiet. The sun began to descend into the west edge of the lake. Even the birds and insects were quiet.

I reached out for Marilyn as the pastor bowed his head to say a short prayer and dismiss the crowd. Still without speaking the people rose, took their blankets or cushions, and went to the big tent for the evening meeting. Holding the towels about Margie and Marilyn, I moved toward the bathhouse, Beverly bringing the younger twins along behind us.

As I rubbed the towel to dry the wet hair, one twin said, "Mother, we were washed clean, weren't we?"

"Yes," I said, "washed clean."

CHAPTER THIRTY-EIGHT

So many times when I took my five children anywhere at least one of them embarrassed me in some way—a different way each time. When I had lived in Three Forks I had taken them with me to church always. Parking all five of them on the front seats, with instructions to Beverly to see that they did not talk, I would go up to the piano for the service. For the first ten or fifteen minutes, during the singing, prayer, response, offertory, when there was interesting activity, they sat straight in their places, Jim's cowlick on the back of his head not even popping up the dampened hair. Then Jim would begin to wiggle. He would slide back and forth in the pew, slowly at first, and gather momentum until he would see me frowning. He could usually find something to move that would squeak, perhaps the little envelope holders on the back of the next pew, until my headshaking stopped him. I think I rarely remembered the words of the sermon. I was so concerned with keeping the children in order—they in their pew alone, I sitting tensely on the rostrum by the piano.

In my work as a teacher of English I often had to direct plays given by the students. We practiced in the evening on the stage in the school gymnasium. Usually I took the children with me, leaving them in chairs near the stage as I paced back and forth calling directions to the students. When Jim and Joan became sleepy I took the children home, telling the actors on stage to go on with their lines while I was gone. After putting my family to bed and leaving the housekeeper in charge, I went back to my play directing. Experiences of this kind gave me some confidence, but the unexpected often happened and my face burned with embarrassment.

At graduation time, since I was senior sponsor, I had to sit on the stage with the officials. I watched the children carefully as they sat in the front row directly below me. The ceremony was long. Jim wearied. He lifted his arms and stretched sleepily. The zipper on the front of his pants suddenly popped open—the whole length—and his white underwear was plainly exposed, contrasting sharply with the dark blue of his trousers. He was totally unaware of this. I fidgeted in my chair, trying not to look at him, but drops of perspiration gathered on my forehead and seeped down the sides of my face. I could feel the nerves jerking in my right leg. Without moving my head I glanced at the people beside me, trying to discover whether they had seen Jim's exposure. No one gave any indication.

There I sat for twenty minutes until the recessional, played on the borrowed organ, freed me to leave the stage and hurry to Jim. Standing in front of him to hide him a bit, I managed to push in his underwear and close the zipper.

Several years later another incident filled me with chagrin. It was spring. I had bought a new straw hat and a blouse to match which pepped up my old black suit and gave me a sense of gaiety. General Conference was in session, and I wanted to attend at least one day of the meetings. Optimistically I planned to take the children with me. We left home very early in order to get there for the first service. The children were at their best for the first hour. Then began the expected trips to the rest rooms. In the huge Auditorium I dared not turn any one of them loose to find his own way, so I had to get up from my seat and take each child along the ramps, following the arrows that led me to the rest room marked "Ladies." At noon we went to Aunt Ava's house for lunch. Only one of my brood spilled a glass of milk across the tablecloth. All the adults jumped quickly to their feet to avoid having a lapful of milk. Shamefacedly I sopped up the liquid.

We went back to the Auditorium for one more meeting. The children were now getting restless. I whispered, to quiet them, "If you will just be still until this meeting is over we'll go to the Sugar Bowl and have a milk shake—each one of us." This we had never done before!

"Can we sit on the stools beside the counters?" Beverly asked.

I nodded. They sat very still for a few minutes, only wiggling now and then until the last song dismissed us. At the Sugar Bowl we found five stools unoccupied—not together, but two customers obligingly moved over without my asking them. I thanked them as I lifted or helped each child to the high seats, leaving their legs dangling. I wouldn't need a seat. I circulated around the stools, ready for any emergency. The clerk came to stand before me, looking at us questioningly as he set glasses of water before us.

"Milk shakes for each one," I said, "chocolate, I think—okay, kids?"

They nodded.

The long wait for the milk shakes to be prepared disappointed them, but I kept pointing out interesting things to notice. When the foamy beverages came, the children grew excited.

"Put the straw in your mouth and suck," I whispered to Jim. For a few seconds this absorbed their attention. Then Joan stopped sucking and reached awkwardly for her glass of water. Her arm hit her straw and flipped it to the floor, splashing some of the liquid as it went. Grabbing a napkin,

I stooped to wipe up the slop. Jim turned to see what had happened and knocked over his whole milk shake. I was directly below him. The gooey ice cream fell onto the top of my hat and ran down into the turned up brim, over the edge, and onto my new red blouse. I just stood there, my face burning with anger and embarrassment.

After a minute or two, I gained some equilibrium and began to sop up the mess on the floor, telling Beverly and the girls each to give Jim a "suck" of their milk shakes. As soon as I could I hustled the five out of the Sugar Bowl, down the street, and into the car. I took off my ruined hat, looked at it a second, then wrapped it in a newspaper and put it in the trunk of the car.

The children were silent for a few minutes, expecting scolding, I am sure. But I was too disheartened even to scold them. Soon they were chattering and laughing, talking about the many new things they had seen that day.

I firmly resolved never to take them to a restaurant again until they were older, and that was one resolution I kept.

CHAPTER THIRTY-NINE

With the coming of spring, 1946, I had begun to gather courage to try to improve the house and garage. Both needed a coat of paint—several perhaps. I investigated prices for having this painting done. They shocked me, so I asked, "Why not do it myself?" I mulled over this idea for days.

When school was out I picked strawberries for Mr. Shobe in the field next to my mother's place. He paid me one cent a box for picking them, but I could have all berries with imperfections. I made very little money, but I canned—and we ate many quarts of fresh strawberries.

By this time I had bought a Guernsey cow with a new calf and put her in the pasture with Mother's Holstein. I milked both cows in the evening, fed the calves, and took the remainder of the milk. Mother did this in the morning. We had so much milk that we sometimes separated part of it and used the cream on our cereal and for making butter.

The idea of painting the house still tantalized me. I would stand and look up at the gable end of the two-story part of the structure and wonder how I could get a ladder up that high. I went to see a good friend of my mother's to ask advice. He explained primer coats of paint, "boxing" the paint, the kind and quantity to buy. He walked around the house and looked at the windows, the putty cracked and falling, the holes in the wood siding. He explained how to scrape out all the old putty and put on new stuff.

Pope's epigram, "Fools rush in where angels fear to tread," fit me and my project that summer. I bought the paint, the putty, the brushes, borrowed two ladders from the friend, and put on an old shirt that I found hanging in my brother's closet at Mother's house.

My first job was to remove all the loose putty around each windowpane. I spent days scratching, scraping, and putting in little three-cornered metal wedges to hold the glass firmly. After I had gone over each window—balanced precariously on the long ladder so that I could reach the ones of the second-floor bedrooms—I began to apply the putty with the blunt knife made for that purpose, smoothing the thick substance carefully along the edge of the glass. My legs and feet ached from holding myself on the ladder while I used both hands in my work. Five pounds of putty I put on those windows, but I knew the wind would not find so many cracks to blow through next winter.

The next thing I did was to cut small circles of tin from the ends of cans and nail these pieces neatly in place over holes in the siding of the house. Another day used up! Early the next morning I began to apply a thin coat of paint to the putty and to the tin pieces, then let that dry. My arms and shoulders began to be stiff and sore from the unaccustomed stretching and pounding. I simply told them they would have to get accustomed to the work. The children brought their toys and played below me. I talked with them from my perch on the ladder, often telling them stories. In the morning I would paint on the south and west side in the shade, changing to the east and north later in the day.

My friend came over often in the evenings to inspect, advise, and give me instructions. He explained that "boxing" paint meant first stirring the thick lead from the bottom of the big five-gallon pail, then pouring the liquid into a spare pail he had brought—back and forth from pail to pail until the lead and the liquid were thoroughly mixed. My muscles grew stronger. I could lift and pour the large buckets of paint without trembling so much.

When I began to apply this primer coat, I felt that I was accomplishing something. Over and over again I moved the brush back and forth across the siding, the dry, thirsty wood soaking up much of the liquid. I did not get much surface covered in a day, but I worked at it from very early morning until almost dark, taking time out only to cook meals for the children.

When I got to the high gables, the ladder had to be extended as far as it would go. It was very difficult for me to move. Since I dreaded each wrestle with it, I would reach out as far as I could in every direction before I moved it. When I had worked on the high ladder for hours I ached all over, but in the evening, after we had walked home from my mother's where we milked the cows, I would gloat over the improvement that the primer coat had made.

The second coat left a satiny, shiny surface. Now I felt that I was really progressing. I was painting on the north side one afternoon, weary from the work and sweating from the heat. Halfway up the ladder, with paint pail in hand, I slipped and tumbled to the grass below, paint splashing over me, the ladder, and the shrubbery. The children, hearing the fall, came running.

"Mother, are you hurt?" Beverly was there first.

"Only my dignity," I said. "I didn't fall very far. But I am angry because I have spilled and wasted expensive paint. Can you get that little red can of gasoline in the garage, Beverly? I'll try to clean off my hands and arms. These old overalls are stiff with splashed paint already. A little more won't matter."

I stopped work for the day to clean up the mess.

The days went by and became two weeks. All of the house

and the garage had the two coats of paint, their white gleaming in the sunshine. The front porch was white also, with the floor painted a dark gray. I painted the screens with black screen enamel. I was just finishing the front screen door one afternoon when the telephone rang.

"Get it, Beverly, will you?" I said and went on painting. I had had a telephone put in so that Mother could call me easily at any time.

"They want to talk to you," came Beverly's voice in a few moments.

With care, I set the can of black enamel on a newspaper, laid the brush on the top of the can, and went around the house and into the kitchen. It was five minutes or more before I came back to the front porch. Much can happen in a few minutes, I found out.

"Jim," I screamed as I came around the house toward the front.

For a whole minute I just stood there transfixed. On the front porch, Jim leaned against the porch railing, his hands and the front of his pants, the railing, part of the porch floor all daubed with black enamel. The liquid ran down his brush, down his bare arm, and dripped from his elbow. He saw my anger and dropped the brush which splashed onto the railing and off into the rosebushes. I reached him in two jumps, grabbed his shoulders, and dusted off the seat of his pants with a few loud whacks. He began to cry. I did too. The tears of disappointment slipped down my cheeks and I sobbed in weariness.

"I just wanted to help paint," Jim cried.

I took him into my arms, paint and all, sitting there on on the top step of the porch. When I could stop crying, I tried to explain to him why I had spanked him. We got up and went around the house to the garage where I dipped a rag into the gasoline and cleaned the paint from both of us. It was two days later before I had covered up the splotches of black enamel that Jim had put on.

When I was all through, I stood before the shining, white house in its setting of green plants and trees and looked and looked—drinking in its beauty. I walked slowly all around the two-story building and then the garage. The children joined me, fascinated by my spell.

"It's pretty, isn't it, Mother?" Margie said at last.

"I'm glad it's all done," Beverly said matter-of-factly.

"Was it worth it?" I asked aloud. Then I answered myself, "Yes, it was. It's beautiful." And then to the waiting children I turned and said, "Come on, kids; let's go bake a big fat chocolate cake and put fudge frosting on it."

CHAPTER FORTY

The younger twins were six years old that summer. It was time for them to be in the first grade in the fall. For Joan there was no problem. But Jim . . . Very early I had recognized that he was not normal. He was almost three months old before he could hold his head erect without wobbling. Not until he was nine months old could he sit up alone—and then it was a very insecure position for him.

At the time of his father's accident, when I had had to put him entirely on the bottle, Jimmy began to develop an ejectile vomiting. His food—and we tried everything—did not digest well. He cried often, his stomach cramping. For a long time, I put all his food through a sieve, and even then he often vomited. He slept only a few hours at a time, even when he was two and three years old.

By the time that he was eighteen months old I began to be conscious that Jimmy was really not like other children. Joanie was running around the house on eager feet, no longer evidencing any signs of her prematureness. But Jimmy could only pull himself up, hanging on to chairs and davenport, and walk awkwardly beside them. He could say only a few syllables. His lack of coordination was obvious to me.

One day my sister-in-law, Anna, commented on it. "There's something dreadfully wrong with him, Elsie. Have you considered putting him in an institution?"

There's something so cold and remote about the word "institution." It takes all the joy, the warmth, out of living. It reduces a person to an object, a vegetable.

I tried to defend Jimmy's lack of development, but I knew

my explanations were inadequate. They were a mother's natural snatching at anything in defense of her child.

All that day my mind was perplexed with the problem. That night, as I was getting the younger twins ready for bed, I stood a moment in the bathroom doorway with Jimmy in my arms and said silently, "Oh, Lord, what should I do?"

A warmth diffused my whole being and these words came to me: "Do not fear. This boy has a work to do in the church." I did not understand completely, but I was satisfied and my heart was lighter as I went on into the bedroom with Jimmy.

But he was two years old before he could walk, and then he bumped into everything near him.

When he was four I took him to a specialist who, after examining him thoroughly, explained to me about "partial spastics"—children with damage in the motor area of the brain—caused at birth, perhaps; maybe prenatal. The doctor gave several theories about the possible causes of Jimmy's condition: If a premature baby is "blue" even for a few moments after birth, there can be brain damage. With twins, during pregnancy sometimes one baby is deprived of necessary nutrition.

"You must be very patient with him," the doctor said. "Teach him big motions. He will be very uncoordinated. His nerves do not communicate accurately with his muscles. Don't try to teach him fine skills. He will develop very slowly in dexterity—probably always be extremely awkward. But his mind is normal. However, he will have difficulty with his speech."

"Doctor, ought I to put him in an institution for spastic children?"

"No," he said slowly, "I think not. We have only places for complete spastics. If your son were placed there, he would tend to lower himself to the level of these children. It would not be good. He needs to be encouraged to do everything that he can. He is better off in the home. You must give him individual help. It won't be easy, I can promise you that, but it is the best for him."

As I left his office, I felt the doctor had given me a severe life sentence. My shoulders ached beneath the strain. Patience—I had but a small store of this. I was quick and accurate in my movements. I spoke rapidly. It was extremely difficult for me to slow down. How could I train a partially spastic child?

That summer of '46 I pondered much over Jimmy, knowing I must enter him in school. He and Joanie had been going every morning to the kindergarten in the laboratory school during the winter and spring. In June a notice came from the school saying that if I planned to enter them in first grade in September, I must bring them to the school for tests, readiness tests, on a certain date. I did that.

For over an hour the psychologists and counselors tested and examined Jim and Joan. I waited in the office of the principal, not anticipating the traumatizing experience I would go through as a result of the testing. The examiners came into the office where I waited, followed by the twins.

"We want to talk to you, Mrs. Doig—alone," one of them said.

I sent the twins out on the playground. The principal spoke first.

"We can enroll Joan, but not your son," she said, cutting off her words between her teeth with a finality.

"Oh, I can't separate them," I said. "Jimmy depends on Joan."

"Yes, we know," said a psychologist with soft white hair piled on top of her head. "But," she continued, "Jimmy is a hopeless moron—not even a moron, I'm afraid. He'll never learn to read or write. He has very little mind at all. This is quite evident, we've found as a result of the tests we've given him. He must be taught a trade, something he can do with his hands."

Stunned, I looked at the educator. How could one so beautiful be so cruel!

"But he's a partial spastic. I explained that last fall. He's slow, I know, but the doctor said he must train his mind. His muscles and nerves won't ever work well. The doctor told me . . ."

"We're very sorry, Mrs. Doig. You just have a mother's complex. You have persistently refused to face reality. The interview is over." And they left the room.

I fumbled for my purse and stood by the chair for a few moments before I attempted to walk to the door. It was as if I had been given a blow between my eyes; I felt stunned. Yes, I had studied psychology, had taken my degree in education, had been a teacher for a number of years. Of course I could be wrong. But the doctor had told me. . . . Shaking my head to clear my fuzzy thinking, I went out to the playground to get the twins. We went home their favorite route—through the big college stadium which was between the campus and our house.

As I cooked supper, I was hardly aware of the children about me. After we had eaten, I took my mending outside and sat near the big cottonwood tree where the children took turns pushing each other in the swing and playing in the dirt. They did not seem to notice my silence.

When it began to grow dark, we went into the house. I read their evening story, heard their prayers, and when they were ready for bed I kissed each one absentmindedly.

I walked into the living room and stood before the picture of Jim and me—our wedding picture.

"What shall I do now, Jim?" I asked softly. "I don't know what to do." How desolate I felt because he could not answer, could not help me with this problem! For hours I wrestled with my thoughts. I cried and prayed and cried.

All the next day and the next I made the motions of going through my work, my mind beating away at the problem. Somewhere—deep inside me—I believed the doctor—the specialist—and refused to accept the decision of the psychologists and counselors, and their tests. Oh, this was normal, I told myself—just a "mother's complex." But I had observed Jimmy too, watched him very closely after the doctor had talked to me. I knew the odds were against me—six learned counselors against one doctor—and a mother, who could not keep from thinking with her heart. But I kept hearing the doctor's words. Jimmy had finally learned to talk—not well, but he communicated with us in sentences, not just words. His pronunciation was slow and awkward. He had learned to tie his shoelaces—it took him a long time each morning, but he did it. He observed things, remembered them, expressed ideas—haltingly, to be sure, but we could understand him. I worked with him on pronunciation and enunciation.

Day after day I battled with my problem. There was no "special" school for spastics in our town. Besides, when I had talked with the specialist he had advised against entering Jimmy in such an institution.

"Your son is not a complete spastic," he had said, "he's only partially handicapped. If he were associated only with spastics, he would tend to lower himself to their level of capabilities. Keep him in your home. Love him. Be very patient with him, and he'll learn to do most things that any normal boy would do. His thinking mind is there, but it will take longer for him. You will get very discouraged, but you must not give up."

His advice won. I entered Jimmy and Joan in the first grade of the public school. That first year was not a good experience. The teacher sent home very unkind notes. She spanked him several times "because he is so stubborn and refuses to learn." I tried to explain to her about his physical handicap.

The other children in his room were allowed to ridicule him, make fun of his speech, call him "odd ball," "queer duck," "dummy."

One evening Jim came home from school, his shirt torn into rags, his pants and hands dirty, his face bruised.

"Jimmy," I said, "what happened?"

He leaned against the door and the tears ran down his face, washing some of the dirt away.

"They say I'm dumb, so they beat me up," he sobbed.

"Who?"

"The big boys in my room."

I put my arms around him, and we cried together. The next day I tried again to talk to the teacher. She repulsed me. I went to the principal. He was sympathetic but offered no solution.

The next year, when Jimmy was going to repeat the first grade, I went to the school before it opened. I knew how terrible "interfering mothers" could be—especially "teacher-mothers." Somehow I must make this teacher—it was a different one from the year before—see that I was not just defending my son, that I wanted him to face his handicap, but I wanted justice for him. I asked only for understanding.

I had prayed for hours. I had read everything I could

find about spastics. Very humbly I explained my problem and asked this teacher for cooperation.

"I will try to teach him at night whatever he does not learn during the day," I offered. "I'll buy texts just like these at school. But he must have the daily challenge of other youngsters his own age. Besides, I must teach school, too, to earn a living for my children."

The teacher was kind. We talked of ways of supplementing the schoolwork of the day—the part Jimmy did not learn as quickly as the other children did. She offered to send home brief notes telling what he should be taught.

Every night, after we had eaten our evening meal and the girls were washing the dishes, Jim and I struggled with his learning to read, to write, to make figures and count and add. He was naturally left-handed. The other first-grade teacher had attempted to change this. The present teacher was wise enough to let him write with his left hand.

It seemed as if he thought backward, or at least that his actions and words came out backward. He made his numbers upside down and backwards. It took many laborious hours to correct this fault. A seven was ⅃ and a nine was ϱ. Sometimes he cried in discouragement. Often I felt like crying. But we had to keep on.

In learning to count, he was awkward. Even when he tried to tell me of several things he said it backward. "There are four or three kittens in the box," he always said.

I wanted the teacher to know how much I appreciated her patience with my son. At Christmastime I made candy—divinity, fudge, penuche—and sent her a big box of it. On Valentine's Day I sent her red roses. I found out the date of her birthday and had Jimmy take her a lovely handkerchief.

And night after night we labored—Jim and I—trying to

learn to read, to add numbers. Fortunately I had studied primary methods before teaching rural school, where I had taught first grade along with the other grades for six years.

It was not easy—no quick miracle. Jimmy had learned to accept defeat. He gave up too quickly. He was afraid of failing and hesitated to attack anything new. I could not seem to build up within him a sense of confidence. Each new thing was a difficult hurdle, almost a threat to him.

We kept at it, hour after hour. Often I said to myself, "I must be his backbone until he develops one of his own."

Jim had other problems too. He was a bed wetter. This was extremely embarrassing to him. Often at night I would get him up and to the bathroom. It did not seem to help. When he became disturbed emotionally he vomited. Day or night, no matter where we were, he vomited.

Of course, children continued to make fun of him, to imitate his awkward speech, his uneven walk. I would say to myself, "It would be better if he were a true spastic. Then people would recognize his difficulty and not think him just a 'gook,' as he is often called."

In May I waited anxiously for the teacher's decision. Would it be possible for him to try second grade? He was getting so tall. His height was obvious among his classmates. The day before school was dismissed, the teacher called me on the telephone.

"I think he should be passed to the next grade," she said. "It will be difficult, but with your help he can make it."

With deep sincerity I thanked her. After hanging up the receiver, I took a few moments to thank my heavenly Father too.

CHAPTER FORTY-ONE

I had known Wendell for years. He was a friend of the children's father before I had met either one of the two men. Their ranches adjoined, and they had worked cattle together. Wendell had often eaten meals at our house when he was helping to round up cattle or brand them.

One day in 1944 I met Wendell's mother in Manhattan. We visited, and as she started to get into her car she said, "Elsie, why don't you write to Wendell? He needs letters from home. He's been in the South Pacific war area for over a year now, on New Caledonia, I think. His last letter said, 'The native girls don't seem so dark to me now as they did when I first came.'" She laughed but I sensed her concern for his loneliness.

"Here, I'll give you his address." She took a letter from her purse, tore off the left top corner of the envelope, and handed the piece to me.

"I will write," I promised. And I did—not often though, for I had two brothers in the Air Force. I wrote long newsy letters with nonsense in them. I talked of the single girls waiting for the servicemen to come home. I even suggested two that I was sure he knew—asked him to write to them, told him what a good wife each one would make. He wrote back, "I'll choose my own wife, Elsie, if I ever marry."

When the war was over he was still in the Pacific. He waited impatiently for his return to the United States. "Over thirty months here," he wrote. "I'll die of jungle rot if I don't get out of these tropics pretty soon."

Just before Christmas his company was put on board a ship headed for San Francisco. His letters came at irregular intervals. He was discharged from the Army, had to report to his original port of drafting, then was free to return home.

He did not want to go back to the ranch—said he had lost all interest in it—persuaded his father to sell it. He wanted to take advantage of the GI training bill. In January I had a letter that was short: "I'm coming. My train pulls in at 9:30 P.M. Thursday. You'll meet me. I don't know why you ever moved to Missouri anyway. I must see you."

The children were in bed and asleep before I left to go to the depot. Rarely did I leave them alone, but Beverly was almost ten years old. I would be gone only a few minutes. I had called the depot. The train would be on time.

As I stood on the platform near the railroad tracks, I watched the flashing semaphores. I tried to sort out my emotions. Wendell's letters had become more and more serious. I sensed his amorous interest but had warded it off always.

Just then, with a roar and a screech of brakes, the train stopped, the passenger cars near me. The brakeman jumped off and put down the step for his passengers. I saw Wendell standing in the open doorway waiting to be the first one to descend. He came quickly to where I stood, put his free arm around me, and tried to kiss me. I jerked away.

"Look out!" I said. "You'll knock off my hat. Now—just let me look at you. Wow! Am I ever glad to see you! Five years, is it?"

"Almost," he said. "Seems like ages."

I led the way to my car, got in under the wheel. I motioned him to the front seat beside me. He swung his suitcase into the back. We drove silently for a moment.

"Tell me about everyone back home in Montana. I've

missed them so." He talked as I asked questions, naming friends and relatives.

We drove into the driveway and went into the house by the back door, speaking quietly so as not to awaken the children. As soon as we were in the dining room, he set down his suitcase, put both arms around me, and kissed me hard on the mouth.

"There," he said with finality. "I've been wanting to do that for about twelve years. Now, do you understand what I could not put into my letters?"

"I think you're just glad to see an old friend, Wendell."

"You know better than that."

I moved away from him so that I could think unemotionally. My heart was pounding so hard I was sure he could hear it. We sat on the davenport and talked. He told me of the long, lonely days of the war. I talked of the children. It became late.

"Hey! I have to teach school tomorrow—or is it now today?" I said. "You will sleep at Mother's. Come on; I'll take you there. She won't even awaken."

The next morning he drove me to my school and returned to pick me up at four thirty. Beverly and the twins, already home from school, crowded around us as we drove into the yard. They had always known Wendell, a friend of Daddy's. He talked to them, teased them, pushed them in the swing as I cooked supper. We laughed a lot as we ate together, the seven of us around our kitchen table.

The next day was Saturday. We went downtown to the stores where Wendell bought each child a small gift. They were not afraid of him, did not resent him as they had Bert Hartnell. They listened as he told of the customs of the people on the islands of Bora Bora, of New Caledonia, of his flight to Manila, of Papeete. The names were strange to them. He gave us necklaces of seashells made by the darkskinned natives of the islands, telling of one excursion he and another GI had made into a part of an island where no other Army personnel had been. He laughed as he talked of trading cigarettes and candy bars for a "cat's eye" ring, for bookends made of heavy wood, crudely carved in the shape of a head of a native. He gave us the bookends.

Sunday evening we took him to the train and went back to our house, which seemed lacking in one important ingredient of a home.

In the spring he began to write of my coming to Montana to see him. "You can leave as soon as your school is out. I can't. I've taken this job. I'll pay your way. You'd like to see all your friends here. I want to see you."

I wrote him of the house painting, of my garden, of the work I must do. But he was restless and unsettled. A product of five years in the Army, I reasoned.

Anna wrote asking me to come to see their baby. "Nine years I waited for a baby. I was always interested in your children, but then you moved. It was like a miracle when I became pregnant, soon after you left. I can hardly believe it's true even now." And then she added, "Wendell was here all afternoon Saturday. He talked of you most of the time. 'Can't you get Elsie to understand?' he said. 'She's got to marry me. I need her and she needs me.'"

When the house painting was finished I was completely weary. Then one evening when I was milking the cows my brother Sammy drove into Mother's yard.

"Need any help?" he called as he stuck his head in the open door of the barn.

"Nope! Almost through. Say, you can let the Holstein out," I said.

"Hey, Elsie," he said as he helped me turn the cows

loose from their stalls, "how about your going to Montana with me next week? I have to drive up there—some business I must take care of. Also I want to go to the college in Bozeman to check my credits there. I may take some graduate work at Montana State College in the fall. You look kinda peaked. Lost some weight, huh? Have you skinnied up! What you been doing?"

"Painting my house. It was more of a job than I expected," I said. "But it's done now, and I'm glad."

"You need a rest. Come go with me—only be gone a week—two days and a night to go. We'll drive all night, take turns at the wheel. Give us three days there. Then come right back. I need another driver. How about it?"

"But the children? They're too much for Mother."

"Tell you what I'll do. I'm going to Lawrence tomorrow to see Wilmer. I'll ask Alma if she'll take care of them that week. I'm sure she will. She owes you a good turn. Think it over."

I did think. I thought until my head ached. I did not sleep much that night. I brought out all the reasons why I could not go. But I knew I would go. The children were excited about a visit to Auntie Alma's house. Uncle Pedro—as they had always affectionately called him—was their favorite relative. We left them in Lawrence on our way west.

It was late in the evening when we reached Anna's house in Montana. I had not told her or Joe of my coming, but she wasn't much surprised. After greetings, I pushed past them and tiptoed into the baby's room and stood looking down at the sleeping child. I said to Anna, who had followed me in, "Isn't it wonderful?"

We marveled for a few minutes, then turned back to the kitchen.

"Does Wendell know you're here?" Anna asked.

"No, I'll see him tomorrow."

The next morning I went to the ranch to see Wendell's mother—very early. She met me at the gate.

"If you hadn't come, Elsie," she said, "I'd have sent for you. Wendell is on needles and pins."

"I'm going to knock some sense into the head of that son of yours," I said. "He has no business being interested in a widow and her five orphans."

She smiled and shook her head. "He's awful stubborn, you know. Seems to have his mind made up."

I went on over to the town where Wendell was working. It was almost noon when I walked into the store and looked down the aisles until I saw his dark, curly hair, away at the back of the room. Making my way between the counters, I was almost beside him before he saw me. He reached for my hand and pulled me with him to the stock room at the rear. There he held me close in his arms and kissed me, my head pushing against the hard boxes of shoes on the shelves behind me. Then he gave a sigh that seemed to come all the way from his toes.

"So you did come," he said.

"Yes, I came to tell you that this nonsense about our marrying has got to be stopped." And I rallied all the moth-eaten reasons why we could not marry.

He didn't answer for a moment. Then he said. "Well, let's not talk about it right now. Let's just enjoy these hours—how long can you stay? How did you come? Do you need any money? Say—let's get out of here. Time for my lunch hour, anyway."

We went to a restaurant nearby, where we ordered food. When it came, neither of us ate much. His hand shook so that he spilled the soup every time he tried to get a spoonful to his mouth. I laughed at him.

"It's no use, Elsie. You've got to marry me."

"But you know I came all the way to Montana to tell you that I can't."

"I've tried dating girls. They're a dime a dozen, and that's all they're worth. I want someone as old as I am—someone with maturity. The war made us older. I want you."

We left the restaurant and walked around until it was time for him to return to his work.

"I'll be through at six," he said, "be over at Anna's by eight."

For five days we spent all of his free hours together, not leaving many for sleep.

"Elsie, you might as well give up. I'm not taking 'no' for an answer. I'm just as stubborn as you are."

We left it at that when I drove away with Sammy, back to Missouri. The night was hot and humid as we drove up before my little house. I got out, thanked Sammy, took my suitcases and unlocked the back door. I stopped a moment and looked around me. The moon made a soft light that let me see the shining white paint I had worked so hard to apply. The cottonwood tree rustled its leaves gently, and I turned to look at the swing which hung from the big, low branch. How quiet it was without the children! Could I be satisfied with them—just my life with them—any more? Suddenly I knew that I could not. It was foolish to fight it any more. I needed a mate. The children needed a complete family. They liked Wendell. I felt so secure with him. The tension seemed to go out of me. My shoulders that I had held so stiffly erect for six years relaxed and went limp. I sighed contentedly. I went into the house to bed—to sleep—at peace.

The next day, after I had brought the children home, I called Wendell.

"You're right," I said. "I want to marry you."

"You what? Repeat that."

I did.

"You make the wedding arrangements for—say—Saturday night?" he said then.

"Will do," I answered. "Say, this is costing me money. If you are going to support me and the children, you'd better learn how to save money."

"I love you," he said and hung up the receiver.

I turned to explain to the waiting children.

"We're going to marry Wendell. Now we'll be seven again—a complete family." We talked of plans.

After they had gone to bed, I walked about the house, not tired, just exhilarated. I went into the bedrooms and looked at the sleeping children.

"How glad I am," I said to myself, "that I kept them all. I really did have none to give away."